"Abide in me, and I in you. As the branch cannot bear fruit by itself, unless it abides in the vine, neither can you, unless you abide in me"

JOHN 15:4 ESV

# COFFEE FOR ONE

DEVOTIONALS THAT INSPIRE

## SCOTT MICHAEL RINGO

OCEAN GRAND

*To my wife, family, my parents, and grandparents who taught me of Jesus' love for me and modeled an example of believers in community changing the world.*

*To the online community of subscribers of my daily writing who inspired these and were diligent to be a part of the ongoing process for many years.*

*To my children, which makes writing have more purpose as we strive together to be better disciples of Jesus. It is an amazing thought that one day, you can share these with your children and grandchildren.*

*Cover design and book formatting by Scott Michael and Tristan Ringo*

COFFEE FOR ONE

Published by Ocean Grand

Virginia Beach, Virginia

Copyright © 2000 by Scott Michael Ringo

All rights reserved.

Cover Design: Scott Michael Ringo

Photo: Shutterstock

First Edition 2000

Printed in the United States of America.

Permissions

ISBN 978-1-7356637-4-6

eISBN 978-1-7356637-5-3

# CONTENTS

# JOURNALING THROUGH THIS BOOK

## Journal

At the end of each lesson are some questions and journal pages. Journaling is a great way to hear Jesus in what we are learning. It is also a great way to keep a diary of notes, thoughts, and action steps from the lesson. Once the study is finished and the pages filled out, it is a great resource to return to time and time again as we take action to transform our communities and make more disciples of Jesus.

I highly encourage you to take time and listen to Jesus and fill up the journal pages. If you are reading this in an electronic format, you can make digital notes right in the application.

Each chapter has questions at the end that you can use individually to help you journal about what you read, or even with a group.

## About this Book

Being a Christian is entirely different than attending church once a week and a small group study one other night of the week. The early church transformed their neighborhood and the world through making disciples who obeyed the commandments.

I hope you like coffee, because that is the fuel that wrote these studies. I'd like to invite you to pull up a chair and grab your cup of coffee. These studies were developed by writing to thousands of people subscribed to an online community around the world. In response, disciples were made, discussions happened, and lives were changed. These are studies you can work through yourself or with your family, group of friends, or even a small group. However you use them, they will lead you into a deeper discovery of God's role and plan for your life.

## Explanation of Spelling

Throughout this book I have purposely not capitalized the name of satan. I understand that it is a name and in the English language the rules say to capitalize all names. I do not consider satan to be worthy of capitalization and choose to break the grammar rule in order to not capitalize the enemy of which he is.

# INTRODUCTION

What would it be like to walk along the road with Jesus and hear what he taught the disciples? Since creation, God's interest has only and ever been in His creation following and glorifying Him. Throughout history, God has pursued humanity and is now standing face-to-face with a chosen twelve with whom He will change the world.

"Now after John was arrested, Jesus came into Galilee, proclaiming the gospel of God, and saying, "The time is fulfilled, and the kingdom of God is at hand [come near]; repent and believe in the gospel" (Mark 1:14 & 15 ESV).[1] The gospel was readily accessible but what must they do to accept the kingdom of God? Trust Jesus and learn to do what He was doing. Follow Jesus and trust Him even unto death.

Making disciples of this small, unassuming group of twelve men is Jesus' only focus for three years. Success in the kingdom of God is being defined by Jesus Himself as making disciples that make disciples. From this point forward, there is no more guessing how Jesus is building His Church. True disciples are those that abide [follow] His word and glorify God by making many disciples (John 8:31, John 15:8). All that matters from this point forward is obedience to Jesus' word [all that He teaches] as a disciple and making other disciples.

God's direction to us is to glorify Him, be simple and reproduce simple disciples.

The gospel is near...will we accept the gospel?

# ONE

# DIG

The archeology team had been excavating the site for five years in the middle of the dry, parched continent. Just when money was about to dry up and they could move to a more promising site, they would stumble across another piece of pottery. Then "Gold seeker" nonprofits would pour more money into the project and make them captive to the desolate place for another year.

At the beginning of the project, Johnson, the head archeologist, watched reruns of famous historic finds in his mind that he had seen on National Geographic. Each day the team dug, believing that day they would find the most important artifact in history or the foundation of a wall of a great forgotten city that would make them famous. Yet, each day they sifted through yards of sand, while their lives and fame slipped away from them. It did not seem there was a more worthless way to spend one's life than endlessly searching for something was not there to find.

The sun was giving way to night as it slipped over the horizon, and the heat of the day was melting into cool wind.

Another couple shovels of sand and Johnson would soon be resting in his tent for the evening.

"Thud," the shovel hit something and Johnson dropped to his knees and began feeling around in the sand in with his hands. There was an object just under the surface, but the sand kept sifting into the space the shovel had made. Hope became a fire, and with the darkness closing in, the time that during any other day never seemed to end was now precious and slipping away. His mind raced. With barely enough money left on the project to buy food, there had been none to buy batteries for the lamps, nor fuel for the generators. For hours, Johnson and the team gingerly felt in the sand, careful not to move anything before they could take pictures at first light in the morning. Something was interesting just below the sand.

As Johnson sat in the sand all night next to the dig opening, he wondered if tomorrow morning would be when his entire life came together in success.

Humanity has placed great value on old relics and artifacts. Men and women give their entire lives to high-level degrees in archeology and time spent at archeological sites, hoping to discover the past and ancient truths. Nonprofit Foundations pour billions of dollars into archeology and anthropology rather than addressing the current needs of the tens-of-thousands that die daily around the world because of starvation. Still, museums spend more billions to display the artifacts and relics.

Consider our actions and the words we say and how much more valuable they are than the great treasures of the earth. Rarely do we think about how priceless each word is that comes from our mouths or written on a page than all the treasures of the world. In the Bible, James says:

> If we put bits into the mouths of horses so that they obey us, we guide their whole bodies as well. Look at the ships also:

though they are so large and are driven by strong winds, they are guided by a very small rudder wherever the will of the pilot directs. So also the tongue is a small member, yet hit boasts of great things.

How great a forest is set ablaze by such a small fire! And the tongue is a fire, a world of unrighteousness. The tongue is set among our members, staining the whole body, setting on fire the entire course of life, and set on fire by hell (James 3:3-6).

Our words carry with them life or even death. A kind word to another human can make a difference in how their day goes. David writes:

"Anxiety in a man's heart weighs him down, but a good word makes him glad" (Proverbs 12:25).

"A soft answer turns away wrath, but a harsh word stirs up anger" (Proverbs 15:1).

## The Challenge

Archeologists and Anthropologists give their entire lives to "The Dig," to find relics and artifacts that when found are priceless.

Nothing is as valuable or as powerful as our words. The decision to say them, write them, or omit them from human history has an effect on what your impact on the world is. Today, according to experts, if you are a woman you will speak over 25,000 words, and a man will speak 12,000. The challenge is to make each of those words count, not only in a positive way but also to glorify God. No matter whom each of us is, our words count. As a Christian, our words should carry with them the example and message of Jesus, which brings life.

## PONDER AND JOURNAL

Take time and ponder these questions. If you are studying this with a group, these are great discussion questions. Write your thoughts in the journal pages.

1. What do the verses above tell us about God?

2. Explain the difference between a harsh and kind word.

3. Do you think most people place the weight that James puts on words?

4. Do the verses in Proverbs describe you? What does their likeness to you tell you about yourself?

5. What can you do to place more value and attention to the words you use?

6. Who can you share this story with this week?

# Journal Pages

This is a great opportunity to journal what you are learning or the action steps you want to take based on this lesson. Doing so will keep all your notes and journaling in this book as future reference. Start by taking a few minutes to pray and ask Jesus to bring to light all you are learning and what transformational changes you can make in your life. If you are reading this in an electronic version, make a digital note and journal.

_____

_____

_____

_____

_____

_____

_____

_____

_____

_____

_____

_____

_____

_____

_____

_____

_____

_____

_____

_____

_____

_____

_____

_____

_____

_____

# Journal Pages

# TWO

# LETTERS

The news hit him hard and rather unexpected. He had never felt like there was anything wrong with the relationship he had with his father, but also never felt like there was anything deep between them. Since he had heard the news, the relationship they did not have seemed more important, though nothing could be different now. As he drove the half-day to make the arrangements and attend the funeral, he wondered if his father had felt the same about him.

He had a great childhood, and his mother and father were both active in raising him. As he drove, every childhood memory came pouring back into his mind in vivid color. His father made it to every baseball game he played and although he played outfield most of the time, made him feel he was the most important player. Their family spent weekends together doing cool family outings, and summer vacations were always the best. He did not remember a single friend who had such involved or engaged parents in their life as his parents had been in his.

Since leaving for college, his relationship with his father changed, but he thought many times it was just part of growing up. They still talked several times a month and kept up with the news. He had longed to move back closer to his parents, but the jobs never worked out to allow it.

Arriving at his parents' house, his mother ran to meet him at the car, her face swollen from the hours of crying. They made the arrangements, and the funeral went as well as a funeral could go. He would spend a week with his mother going through the house and the family business, then back home.

The day after the funeral, he was sitting in his father's study looking over the great number of books his father had amassed. His father, being a writer, loved books and his collection was impressive. He noticed an out-of-place shoe box up on the top shelf of one bookcase. Getting the box, he sat back down in his father's leather chair and carefully opened it. The box was filled with unopened letters written by his father, and every one of them was addressed to his son. Pouring through each love letter his father had meticulously penned to him answered all the questions he had on his drive just days before. Though the distance in miles had increased in their life, their love for each other remained inseparable.

Like the man in the story, our father and creator has left us a stack of love letters. Throughout history, our father God has handcrafted an amazing collection of letters referred to as the Bible to guide, train, and let us know of His unconditional love for us.

Many times, like the man in the story, we may feel like our choices or circumstances have taken us many miles away from God. Many feel that God has never been close to them or does not care if they even exist. Yet, to hear God's voice speaking to us is as simple as opening any of these letters and reading about His love for us.

Occasionally I happen across a letter that someone wrote to me I tucked away in a safe place. When reading the letter again, I am reminded of the special friendship that I have with that person. Letters hold a very special meaning, sometimes more than even spoken words, because the person took the time to write them so we could rediscover them and remember their words.

The Bible, that God has written to us, is hundreds of letters all tucked away waiting for us to discover them and the amazing love story that God has created us for. If you ever wonder if God loves you and cares for you, open the Bible and read any of the hundreds of letters He has written to you.

Throughout the ages, some say that the Bible is hard for the average person to understand and must be taught by skilled professionals. In different times in history, they have taken away the Bible from the common person as a book too complicated for laypersons to understand. Yes, the Bible is a book the most educated scholar can read their entire life and never become bored. But, the Bible God wrote to each of us is easily understood by common people.

## The Challenge

Like the man in the story, many of us wonder occasionally if our Father remembers that we exist. Sometimes it feels like God may be galaxies away, or may not care about us anymore. satan[1] wants us to forget that God painstakingly wrote His story and love for us in hundreds of letters, so we might never doubt His love for us.

Find a few minutes today and every day to pour over some letters that God wrote for you as a reminder that no matter how far God may sometimes feel, His voice is as close as those letters to you. In one letter, Deuteronomy 31:8 Moses tells Joshua, "It is the LORD who goes before you. He will be with you; he will not leave you or forsake you. Do not fear or be dismayed."

## PONDER AND JOURNAL

Take time and ponder these questions. If you are studying this with a group, these are great discussion questions. Write your thoughts in the journal pages.

1. What does it tell us about God that He would write hundreds of letters to us?

2. How was the Bible written?

3. Do you think the entire Bible applies and applies to your life?

4. Think about your diligence to read the Bible, God's letters to you. What does your diligence tell you about yourself?

5. Like the man in the story, how can you rediscover the hundreds of letters God had written all tucked away waiting for you to discover them?

# Journal Pages

This is a great opportunity to journal what you are learning or the action steps you want to take based on this lesson. Doing so will keep all your notes and journaling in this book as future reference. Start by taking a few minutes to pray and ask Jesus to bring to light all you are learning and what transformational changes you can make in your life. If you are reading this in an electronic version, make a digital note and journal.

# Journal Pages

# THREE

# SILK ROAD

The region separating China from Europe and Western Asia is known as the Taklimakan Desert or the "Land of Death." There is little there other than sand, sandstorms, and more sand. There is little rainfall and almost no oases. It was across this barren land that early Hans explorers traveled looking for objects of worth and beauty for their emperor. Through expeditions and individual traders crossing this desert region, the route known as the "Silk Road" was formed.

Rather than a single route, different branches passed through oasis settlements. The routes started from Changan, the capital, and went to the edge of the Taklimakan Desert. From there it took the shortest routes to other areas, and eventually Europe. All along its route, traders and merchants traded the goods from their countries for others. If there was a particular area that became dangerous the route shifted around the threat to avoid it and merged back into where it was safe. The Silk Road carried commodities other than just silk from the East. Caravans to China carried gold, precious metals, ivory, and precious stones. The caravans to the West bartered furs, ceramic, jade, bronze, and silk. All along the route items might change hands several times before reaching the end of its journey.

Goods traveled slowly across Asia on the way to their new destination, and other cultures and religions influenced the merchants along the route. The most influential commodity traded along the Silk Road was indeed religion. They introduced Buddhism to India along the route. We can only speculate at the large significance and influence The Silk Road had on the world across a harsh and dangerous land.

The Silk Road as it was then is much like the pilgrimage we are on now. Life is a series of travels across many terrains. Some terrains are lush and peaceful. Other times the terrain of life seems like endless sandstorms and deserts with few oases. We too are traders who travel across this earth looking for objects of worth and beauty and commodities such as knowledge and wisdom. As each of us travels through life, we carry with us the "goods" we have gained and use them to barter for others. Throughout our lives and at the end, what we have bartered and placed value on will show what matters most for us. For many, what they thought were riches will turn out to only be sand sifting through their fingers.

King Solomon was the wisest and richest man that has or will ever live. Just after God established Solomon's rule as king, He told Solomon to ask for whatever he wanted and God would grant it. Solomon, who could have asked for anything, asked God for wisdom (1 Kings 3:9-14). Solomon writes the same advice for us in Proverbs.

My son, if you receive my words
    and treasure up my commandments with you,
    making your ear attentive to wisdom
    and inclining your heart to understanding;

yes, if you call out for insight
and raise your voice for understanding,
if you seek it like silver
and search for it as for hidden treasures,
then you will understand the fear of the Lord
and find the knowledge of God.
For the Lord gives wisdom;
from his mouth come knowledge and understanding;
he stores up sound wisdom for the upright;
he is a shield to those who walk in integrity,
guarding the paths of justice
and watching over the way of his saints.
Then you will understand righteousness and justice
and equity, every good path;
for wisdom will come into your heart,
and knowledge will be pleasant to your soul;
discretion will watch over you,
understanding will guard you,
delivering you from the way of evil,
from men of perverted speech, who forsake the
paths of uprightness
to walk in the ways of darkness,
who rejoice in doing evil
and delight in the perverseness of evil,
men whose paths are crooked,
and who are devious in their ways (Proverbs 2:2-15).

Nothing is more precious than wisdom and understanding among the items of life that we barter for.

The Challenge

Since the formation of the world, humanity has searched and risked its life to gain the most precious commodities. The Silk Road is only one example of the lengths of which humanity has gone to gain perceived riches. Thousands upon thousands of explorers have lost their lives searching for treasures. Hundreds of thousands, if not millions of business people have lost their families and everything hunting for wealth and long life. Yet, Solomon's words have been around for almost three thousand years, giving us the treasure map to all the riches.

> Blessed is the one who finds wisdom,
>> and the one who gets understanding,
>> for the gain from her is better than gain from silver
>> and her profit better than gold.
> She is more precious than jewels,
>> and nothing you desire can compare with her.
> Long life is in her right hand;
>> in her left hand are riches and honor.
> Her ways are ways of pleasantness,
>> and all her paths are peace.
> She is a tree of life to those who lay hold of her;
>> those who hold her fast are called blessed (Proverbs 3:13-18).

By pursuing wisdom, God promises us long life in one hand, riches and honor in the other, the tree of life, happiness, and complete satisfaction. Wisdom gives us everything, why not pursue her?

Take time and ponder these questions. If you are studying this with a group, these are great discussion questions. Write your thoughts in the journal pages.

1. What does Proverbs 3:13-18, written by the richest man who will ever live, tell us about God?

2. How valuable is wisdom and understanding in the world today?

3. If more people had the wisdom and understanding Solomon speaks about, what would this world be like?

4. What does Proverbs 3:13-18 tell you about yourself? Do you have a long life in one hand, riches and honor in the other, the tree of life, happiness, and complete satisfaction?

5. How can you find wisdom and get understanding and is the one who finds wisdom, the gain better than silver and her profit better than gold?

6. Do wisdom and understanding come from the Bible or do you get it somewhere else?

# Journal Pages

This is a great opportunity to journal what you are learning or the action steps you want to take based on this lesson. Doing so will keep all your notes and journaling in this book as future reference. Start by taking a few minutes to pray and ask Jesus to bring to light all you are learning and what transformational changes you can make in your life. If you are reading this in an electronic version, make a digital note and journal.

_____

_____

_____

_____

_____

_____

_____

_____

_____

_____

_____

_____

_____

_____

_____

_____

_____

_____

_____

_____

_____

_____

_____

_____

# Journal Pages

# FOUR
## BRIDE

The day had finally come, one that she had been waiting for all of her life. Well, she had been waiting all her life, but eagerly waiting for this particular day since she was six years old. When she was six, there was a magical day one spring when her mother had taken her to a bridal shop to be fitted for a flower girl's dress for her aunt's wedding. That day, as the new dress slipped over her head, life had a purpose. Life was not as much about playing dolls and getting dirty in the yard anymore, though those activities still held meaning. It was about preparation for something bigger, much bigger. As she stood there looking at that beautiful dress, her feet moved almost on their own as she made a small twirl, her eyes never leaving the mirror. An incredible awakening happened in her mind just moments later as she saw her aunt.

She ran out of the dressing room to show her aunt the beautiful dress she had just tried on. As she hurriedly turned the corner, her aunt was standing in an open room filled with light and a soft white glow. In the middle of the room, her aunt was standing on a platform with mirrors all around her, wearing the most incredible cloud of white. The wedding dress flowed to the floor, covered with glistening jewels and lace. She had never seen her aunt look so radiant, and even her face had a new expression on it. Since that day, life would never be the same and everything seemed to pull her towards the day she too would stand adorned in her own dress on her wedding day.

The day had come, though it had seemed like an eternity since the day she was six. As the doors before her opened, she looked down the rows of people to the other end of the aisle. There at the end of the aisle was the love of her life, waiting in all his splendor to marry her. The day had come.

Have you ever seen a little girl's eyes light up when she puts on a Cinderella dress? With the dress on, she spins and dances, gliding from place to place. There is even more excitement when an older or grown woman tries on a wedding dress, her whole behavior changes. Like the little girl, she spins, her face is aglow, her step is different, and she even feels more special. I watched this portrayal backstage at a church. A friend was in a drama for Father's Day, and she was playing the daughter grown up and was getting married. Though she is already married, with the wedding dress on she was beaming as if it was her wedding day. To look at her face made me and everyone else excited. It was easy to go back to the day she married and imagine her excitement and the radiance she must have felt on that day.

We too as the Church, like the bride and the little girl in the story, should wait with incredible anticipation for the day that we meet Jesus. We are His bride, and since the first day that we glimpse His love life should take on preparation for something bigger, much bigger. Though we must live through this life, this life is merely a preparation and a time to help others in their preparation to spend eternity with the Trinity.

We, as the Bride of Christ, get to try on a wedding dress

every day of our life. Every day we prepare ourselves as a bride to Jesus, who will be our bridegroom. What we do each day, and how we do it, should reflect our excitement, anticipation, and purpose of our soon and coming wedding day with Christ. For the little girl, dolls and playing in the yard did not have as much meaning anymore once she caught a vision of the bigger story. In the Christian's life, the activities of the world should pale compared to living a life engaged and promised to the Creator and Lord of all and preparing ourselves for Him.

In Revelation 19, John writes of the day the "doors open," and we see Christ at the end of the aisle waiting for us:

> Then I heard what seemed to be the voice of a great multitude, like the roar of many waters and like the sound of mighty peals of thunder, crying out,
> "Hallelujah!
> For the Lord our God
> the Almighty reigns.
> Let us rejoice and exult
> and give him the glory,
> for the marriage of the Lamb has come,
> and his Bride has made herself ready;
> it was granted her to clothe herself
> with fine linen, bright and pure"—
> for the fine linen is the righteous deeds of the saints
> (Revelation 19:6).

## The Challenge

Perhaps only women will experience the unexplainable thrill on earth to walk down an aisle to meet their groom after having waited for that moment all their lives. Likewise, men watch with amazement as their bride walks down the aisle to join herself to him as one. As Christians, we all will get to experience the thrill of walking down the aisle to meet our bridegroom, Christ. Our lives should be passionately pulled toward our wedding day with Christ more than any other force that affects us. We should be passionate about our preparation for that wedding day and passionate about helping others prepare for their wedding day. It is time that we as Christians stop being drawn in by the world's tactics to be pursuers of material possessions and lesser lovers. Christ, waiting at the end of this life to be our bridegroom, should be our only passion and focus. The day has come.

## PONDER AND JOURNAL

Take time and ponder these questions. If you are studying this with a group, these are great discussion questions. Write your thoughts in the journal pages.

1. What does Revelation 19:6 say about the fine linen with which the church clothes herself? What does that tell us about God?

2. If you are a woman, have you experienced the excitement of your wedding day? If you are a man, have you experienced the excitement of a bride on her wedding day?

3. Do you think understanding this verse helps pull us toward our wedding day with Christ and ignite a passion for our preparation for that wedding day?

4. When you read this, what do your emotions about this verse tell you about yourself?

5. How can you be helping others prepare for their wedding day with Christ?

5. The great multitude says, "...his Bride has made herself ready" (Revelation 9:6). How can you be working to make yourself ready for your marriage to Jesus?

# Journal Pages

This is a great opportunity to journal what you are learning or the action steps you want to take based on this lesson. Doing so will keep all your notes and journaling in this book as future reference. Start by taking a few minutes to pray and ask Jesus to bring to light all you are learning and what transformational changes you can make in your life. If you are reading this in an electronic version, make a digital note and journal.

# Journal Pages

---
---
---
---
---
---
---
---
---
---
---
---
---
---
---
---
---
---
---
---
---
---
---
---
---
---
---
---
---
---
---
---

# FIVE
## UNIQUE

What are your passions? It may take a minute to sort out what your passions are. It is not a question a person gets asked a lot. Many ask how we are, or how we feel, but usually not questions that probe as deep as our passions.

Growing up, I adopted a belief that anything that had to do with passions was wrong. I did not understand it is what you do with the passion that determines whether it is right or wrong. God made passion, and He made the passions we each have. Many of my junior years I was trying to suppress passions that God was trying to bring to life inside me. He made those passions and desires to help guide me in what He has called me to do.

God cares about your passions because He put them there to guide you through your life in how He made you. God does care that you enjoy what you do, where you live, and how you spend your free time. He made you unique, and He wants you to enjoy that uniqueness. David responds to God in Psalms 139:13-15:

You made all the delicate, inner parts of my body and knit me together in my mother's womb. Thank you for making me so wonderfully complex! Your workmanship is marvelous- and how well I know it. You watched me as I was being formed in utter seclusion, as I was woven together in the dark of the womb. You saw me before I was born. Every day of my life was recorded in your book (Psalms 139:13-15).

Those delicate inner parts that God knit together to make you include your emotions, your likes, your dislikes, even what you enjoy for fun.

All of us have times in our lives where we feel we are worth nothing and everything is going wrong. Some of us may have those times of defeat more often than others. When David's enemies were hunting him, and he was feeling down about his life and his choices he remembered that God made him unique. David also took comfort in knowing that God had already planned the very day that he was living.

## The Challenge

Take a moment and respond to God that you are thankful that He made you as you are. God has some radical adventures planned out for you to experience and enjoy in your life. God has today completely planned for you. Next time you are feeling down about yourself or your decisions, remember God made you and your passions as unique as anyone else's. Make it a point to enjoy who you are. Take some time today doing something unique to you and that you are passionate about.

# PONDER AND JOURNAL

Take time and ponder these questions. If you are studying this with a group, these are great discussion questions. Write your thoughts in the journal pages.

1. What does Psalms 139:13-15 say about God's involvement in making you?

2. What does science teach us about our formation, and how does that differ from what we read here?

3. Do you think God made each of your body parts?

4. How does it make you feel to know you were not merely a result of science but God made all of you?

## Prayer

God, we often overlook how involved you are in our lives. Culture tries to convince us you do not exist or are busy on important activities. Yet, we see here in your own words to David that you have known me from before I was born and made each part of me exactly how you want me. Help me to see and remember that you love me and care what happens to me.

# Journal Pages

This is a great opportunity to journal what you are learning or the action steps you want to take based on this lesson. Doing so will keep all your notes and journaling in this book as future reference. Start by taking a few minutes to pray and ask Jesus to bring to light all you are learning and what transformational changes you can make in your life. If you are reading this in an electronic version, make a digital note and journal.

_____

_____

_____

_____

_____

_____

_____

_____

_____

_____

_____

_____

_____

_____

_____

_____

_____

_____

_____

_____

_____

_____

_____

_____

_____

# Journal Pages

## SIX
## WHITE STONE

Most of us enjoy getting special gifts for no particular reason. A gift we get when somebody thinks about us during part of their day and picks us up something special. The value of the gift is not important. Even a gift from the dollar store is grand. When others have those types of thoughts about us, it makes our day light up. We feel special when someone thinks of us enough to put just a little energy into helping us understand their thoughts.

There is a special gift that God has prepared and is waiting until we get to heaven to give it to us. It might be perhaps the most special gift, other than the gift of life forever in heaven. God has prepared a white stone for each of us with a name on it. The name on the stone is a name only He knows and the name one lover calls another in private because it reveals something intimate about their relationship. Revelation 2:17 says:

He who has an ear, let him hear what the Spirit says to the churches. To the one who conquers I will give some of the hidden manna, and I will give him a white stone, with a new name written on the stone that no one knows except the one who receives it.

We have the most passionate of lovers waiting for us every day to romance us. We forget and think that our identity, even our capacity to receive gifts from God comes from our merit. We stay caught up in the thought of striving for everything we want or need; even our daily search for love. The most romantic lover of all is waiting for us, yet we try to find other places that we would rather be. These other places are abiding places, not of God, that we go to find comfort and belonging. We often wander from place to place, thing to thing, and are never fulfilled. In John 15, Jesus tells us we must stay with Him and Him only. "Abide in me, and I in you. As the branch cannot bear fruit by itself, unless it abides in the vine, neither can you, unless you abide in me" (John 15:4). We must make our home with Jesus and He will make His home in us. We must stop wandering and realize that our identity comes from "staying at home" and not trying to fill the void in other ways. It may be surprising, but holiness also comes not out of doing, but staying at home. Our actual home, which is in Christ, remains in us if we remain in Him. Instead of going from place to place searching for love and fulfillment, we already have the fulfillment for which we are looking. Our home, our love, and our fulfillment is Christ who is in us.

## The Challenge

Take a moment and reflect on what you engage in when you feel lonely. Is there a particular place that you go when you need fulfillment? Do you use a substance to give you temporary relief from the thoughts that trouble you? If the answer to any of those questions is anything but Christ, then there is splendid news. Christ can and wants to be the answer to every one of those. Nothing is more satisfying than the author and creator of your life who is Jesus Himself.

Nothing sounds as good to us as when someone knows and uses our name. God has a name like no other for you. He has a special name that He calls you as His lover that only He and you know. In those times of loneliness, despair, or trouble, listen carefully and you will hear your ultimate lover God calling you by name to Him. Go to Him and find true fulfillment.

## PONDER AND JOURNAL

Take time and ponder these questions. If you are studying this with a group, these are great discussion questions. Write your thoughts in the journal pages.

1. What does Revelation 2:17 say about the significance of God giving us a white stone and a new name?

2. Do you think God is a romantic lover of humans?

3. What do you think the hidden manna, the new name, and white stone represent?

4. Have you ever wished you had a different name? What would you name yourself and why?

5. How does it make you feel to know that God has chosen a new name to reward you with when you endure to the end?

# Journal Pages

This is a great opportunity to journal what you are learning or the action steps you want to take based on this lesson. Doing so will keep all your notes and journaling in this book as future reference. Start by taking a few minutes to pray and ask Jesus to bring to light all you are learning and what transformational changes you can make in your life. If you are reading this in an electronic version, make a digital note and journal.

_____

_____

_____

_____

_____

_____

_____

_____

_____

_____

_____

_____

_____

_____

_____

_____

_____

_____

_____

_____

_____

_____

# Journal Pages

# SEVEN

# LEASHES

Each morning I start my day thanking God for the peace and freedom that I have in Him from all entanglements. On one particular morning, while enjoying that thought, a neighbor was walking his dog. Dressed in a tie for work, he patiently waited for his animal to do the things that dogs do on walks. The dog sniffed the grass, deposited some items, checked out a flower, and rolled in the grass. I realized how different the dog on a leash acted than how God created it to be. If the dog were not on the leash, it would be running, rolling, dashing off, and possibly never come back. I wondered who was actually on the leash, the dog or the owner.

Pondering why the leash was necessary, a couple of thoughts came to mind. It may be necessary to domesticate dogs in captivity. Domesticating a dog means training it to be a little less like a dog and a little more like a human. Domesticating also involves training the human to be a little more mindful that the dog has needs and will never be human. We as humans keep animals in an unnatural environment, indoors, and in the box we call home, which is "our" comfort level. We want companionship at a level convenient for us, which causes unnatural rules and behavior for the animals we keep.

Jesus blended into the common people and met them where they were, bringing freedom to the captive. For people like a blind man at a city gate, a woman at a well, a man that had been dead for three days, Jesus gave them all they had ever wanted. From what we know of Jesus' daily life, he had no set schedule; instead, as He went about His day, He gave the people He came across their hearts' desires. Jesus did not have a special appearance but looked like those who were common. The Bible has several accounts where Jesus slipped away into the crowds when the religious leaders were looking for Him. Jesus must have looked like almost any other Rabbi.

When was the last time that we gave someone their hearts' desire because they asked for it? No leashes, no laws, no stipulations, only that which they want more than anything else and everything to carry out that desire. Have you received your hearts' desire of late? I wonder if when we do things for people we do them with only our agenda and goals in mind. Do we only do for others, so we get something out of it ourselves?

Jesus' message to the religious rulers of his time was that they were only thinking of themselves and not the people they were serving. In Luke 11:46 Jesus tells the religious leaders, "You load people down with rules and regulations, nearly breaking their backs, but never lift even a finger to help." It is interesting that it was the common people who recognized Jesus for whom He was and the religious leaders, full of biblical knowledge, who nailed Jesus to a cross.

### The Challenge

Is it possible for us to make an acquaintance with a person with our only motive being to serve them with what they need and want, never mentioning our position, our knowledge, or our needs? Meeting human needs was a daily activity that Jesus the Son of God was consistent with and still is today. The religious leaders were full of book knowledge, but when meeting human needs, they crushed the people beneath religious demands but were never willing to help. Will you be a person who becomes a common person, not bound up in religious laws and controls, and instead brings freedom to those who are in need of a miracle? Be a person who makes your daily activities meeting human needs, giving God glory through your serving.

# PONDER AND JOURNAL

Take time and ponder these questions. If you are studying this with a group, these are great discussion questions. Write your thoughts in the journal pages.

1. What are a couple of differences in animals or even people when they are free or controlled?

2. How could the world be if everyone respected the other and interacted in a non-controlling manner?

3. How have religious leaders or other Christians made you feel like those who Jesus rebukes in Luke 11:46?

4. How can you be more like Jesus and meet people where they are and bring them their heart's desire?

5. Do you blend in with the common people or do you need attention?

6. Can you give Jesus your schedule and allow Him to make interruptions throughout the day meeting other people's needs?

7. Who is someone you can give freedom to that might feel controlled?

# Journal Pages

This is a great opportunity to journal what you are learning or the action steps you want to take based on this lesson. Doing so will keep all your notes and journaling in this book as future reference. Start by taking a few minutes to pray and ask Jesus to bring to light all you are learning and what transformational changes you can make in your life. If you are reading this in an electronic version, make a digital note and journal.

_____

_____

_____

_____

_____

_____

_____

_____

_____

_____

_____

_____

_____

_____

_____

_____

_____

_____

_____

_____

_____

_____

_____

# Journal Pages

# EIGHT

## MINUTES

What is the significance of a minute in a day? How important are ten minutes in a day? We each get 1440 minutes in a day and most of those go by unaccounted for. Sure, we notice the day goes by because we live through each one of them, but it is difficult to account for every one of those minutes in detail. It can be a struggle when someone asks us what we did yesterday to come up with an answer that seems worthy of spending a whole day on the tasks we performed.

According to world statistics, in the last ten minutes, seventy-five mothers gave birth to cute, cuddly babies that are alive and well. In the last ten minutes, forty-two people said their last goodbye to the life that they lived on this earth, content or not with what they had done. For that last group of people, those last ten minutes were important. The last ten minutes were important for all of us if we get practical about it. Medically, it takes fewer than five minutes from the time our hearts stop until we are in eternity. What about spiritually? How long does it take your "spiritual heart" to die once your passions die? It might take even fewer than the last ten minutes.

In John 15:7 Jesus tells us, "If you abide in Me, and My words abide in you, you will ask what you desire, and it shall be done for you." The Greek word used for desire here is, "aijtevw". Aijtevw means to ask, beg, call for, crave, desire, or require. This intense emotion is in the New Testament 68 times. Jesus lived this life of desire (aijtevw) while He walked this earth. Jesus came determined to give everyone He met the desire for what they longed for.

If we believe what Jesus said, then we should be living each minute of every day continually in Jesus, His words continually in us, and doing our best to meet the aijtevw others have.

### The Challenge

Meeting the needs that other people have, shows them that we care for them and that they are important. Each of us, with a little effort, has the ability to meet the needs of others. We might find we have no time to meet the needs of others because we are so busy trying to meet our own wants. You can never give too much to others, and in giving you may just find that you meet your own needs by serving others in their needs.

Take a couple of minutes today and plan out how you can serve those God placed around you by helping them get what they need. The couple of minutes that you give to those around you today could be the biggest difference anyone has made in their life.

## PONDER AND JOURNAL

Take time and ponder these questions. If you are studying this with a group, these are great discussion questions. Write your thoughts in the journal pages.

1. Do you think most people place much emphasis on Jesus' statement to abide in Him?

2. Many people believe that Jesus answers prayer. When these same people need something from Jesus do they ask, beg, call for, crave, desire, or require as the Greek word means?

3. What do you think asking, begging, and requiring from Jesus looks like?

4. How significant were the last ten minutes for you reading this devotional and pondering it?

5. How do you feel when someone cares for you?

6. How can you spend ten minutes today and serve someone by helping them fill a need?

# Journal Pages

This is a great opportunity to journal what you are learning or the action steps you want to take based on this lesson. Doing so will keep all your notes and journaling in this book as future reference. Start by taking a few minutes to pray and ask Jesus to bring to light all you are learning and what transformational changes you can make in your life. If you are reading this in an electronic version, make a digital note and journal.

_____

_____

_____

_____

_____

_____

_____

_____

_____

_____

_____

_____

_____

_____

_____

_____

_____

_____

_____

_____

_____

_____

_____

_____

# Journal Pages

# NINE

## TIKI

My mother has an African lovebird named Tiki who she has had for over seven years. Tiki has lived a lonely life for most of the time my mother has had him. Each time someone would try to pick him up, to hold him, clean his cage, or most anything that got his or her hand remotely close to him, he would attack. His attacks are not little pecks; they are ravenous, vulture-like kill strikes. When something got near him, he would attack with everything his few ounce body had, most of the time drawing blood. Tiki saw everything as an unknown and a threat, resulting in a life missing much love he could have had.

Several months ago, returning home from being out to dinner with my father, my mother found Tiki close to death. His body was limp, and he was barely breathing. That night she held him all night long, as he did not have the strength to fight. A trip to the doctor revealed that Tiki had a heart attack and his liver was not doing well either. The doctor prescribed medicine for his liver that someone had to give him through a dropper each night with a diagnosis that he would most likely not live many days. Weak and frail, each night we held him to give him his medicine. As the days went by, Tiki got better and amazed the doctor by regaining a full recovery.

Now Tiki loves people picking him up and holding him and sits much of the day waiting and watching for someone to reach down, so he can jump up on to their hand. Rarely does he want down, and nor does he bite. Tiki has learned that what he wanted all those years was right in front of him, what he saw as a threat instead was love.

Many have discovered that we are much like Tiki. Some of us have longed for genuine love and intimacy only to attack it bitterly, thinking it would hurt us when it showed itself. The greatest of all these lovers wanting to show us intimacy is God, the creator of us. He has waited patiently throughout history for each one of us to notice Him as our lover and allow Him to engulf us in his arms of love and security. No intimacy can be greater than with the one who made us who knows exactly what we long for. Yet, we have held Him off at great distances, believing that He would hurt us if we allowed Him to get close. We could not have been more wrong in our assumptions.

In Jeremiah 31:3 God told Jeremiah, "Yes, I have loved you with an everlasting love; Therefore with loving-kindness I have drawn you". God was speaking to the Israelites through the prophet Jeremiah. God had pursued His chosen people for thousands of years, only to have them worship His creation instead of Him.

> Have you never heard or understood? Don't you know that the LORD is the everlasting God, the Creator of all the earth? He never grows faint or weary. No one can measure the depths of his understanding (Isaiah 40:28).

God understands that we have all experienced hurt at one

time by love, the church, or another person, and we have attached that hurt to Him. We believe that the hurt came from God when it was only someone acting in His place. God would never hurt us and wants to take each of us into a safe and incredible intimacy with Him. The intimacy that we long for is right in front of us. We have just not realized He has been waiting patiently for us to experience His love.

Even now as I write this, Tiki sits on the table as close as he can get to me and chirps for my attention, wanting me to pick him up and show him affection. If we looked deep inside ourselves, we would also see everything within us wanting to call on God to experience His intimacy.

## The Challenge

Trust God once more and allow Him to heap His lavish love upon you. Do not hold back God with the hurt that you have experienced from humans doing acts in God's name. Find time each day, at whatever cost, and experience the love the creator of the universe has for you. Do not consume the time you spend with Him each day going through religious motions of reading or other actions; instead, just sit and fall deeply in love with your creator, maybe even for the first time.

## PONDER AND JOURNAL

Take time and ponder these questions. If you are studying this with a group, these are great discussion questions. Write your thoughts in the journal pages.

1. What does the verse in Jeremiah 31:3 say about God and His relationship with people?

2. Do you think the Israelites understood the magnitude of God?

3. Do you think people alive today are more or less obedient than the Israelites?

4. Do you believe God loves you with an everlasting love and is drawing you with loving-kindness?

5. How can you trust God's love for you in the future?

# Journal Pages

This is a great opportunity to journal what you are learning or the action steps you want to take based on this lesson. Doing so will keep all your notes and journaling in this book as future reference. Start by taking a few minutes to pray and ask Jesus to bring to light all you are learning and what transformational changes you can make in your life. If you are reading this in an electronic version, make a digital note and journal.

# Journal Pages

# TEN

# VAPOR

With the sunrise, the frost turns a sparkling orange as the waking sun breaks the morning into yet another day. Frosty crystals dance with light in their brief and brilliant life as the sun's warming glow changes them into a soft mist that gently rises from the earth. In one brief moment, creation breathes the first breath of the new day, granting yet another day to many, while some left yesterday. The song of morning again creation sings and does not forget His ancient melody that has been playing since time began. A whisper of wonder and of awe repeated each morning since that light glistened the first morning of creation.

Water comes in many forms and all of them have a beauty of their own. The ocean waves crashing on the shore soothe the ears and the sound runs through the mind like a gentle wind. Mist rising from the earth in the morning brings serenity to the eyes, and its fragrance calms the spirit with tranquility. Beautifully fallen snow sparks the imagination as it clings to the trees and smooths the landscape into gently rolling hills. Gentle raindrops falling bring curtains that beckon sleep, each drop bringing peace and relaxation to the busy world it falls on.

Water, regardless of its form, comes to continue life by giving of itself, so that life around it can live. Water brings life to all it touches and refreshment to the parched and weary. As water, in its different forms, fill brief moments of time, so do our lives.

> Come now, you who say, "Today or tomorrow we will go into such and such a town and spend a year there and trade and make a profit"— yet you do not know what tomorrow will bring. What is your life? For you are a mist that appears for a little time and then vanishes. (James 4:13-14).

As real and tangible as the world seems, it is but a vapor. For each of us, it is here today, but one day will be gone. God promises to create a new heaven and a new earth for us that will remain forever. That life and earth to come is the life we long for, though this one has ineptly taken its place.

While we are here on this earth, we are to fulfill the same role as the different forms of water. We are to bring life to all that our lives touch and refreshment to the parched and weary. We are to pour out our lives in service daily so those around us will have life, in not only this world but also the new one to come.

By using the brief moments that we have now to bring life and promise to those around us, we like the water will be beautiful in all our forms.

## The Challenge

Allow God to transform your life into a gift that is as uniquely beautiful as the forms of water, bringing life to all that it touches. As you allow God to use your life as water pouring out on this earth, do not hold on to the temporary that is just a mist. Instead, hold on to the promise of the life that you will have in a new and perfect world to come. You are beautiful in all the forms that God makes your life, for through your sacrifice others can hear His ancient melody that is still playing since time began.

## PONDER AND JOURNAL

Take time and ponder these questions. If you are studying this with a group, these are great discussion questions. Write your thoughts in the journal pages.

1. Do you think most people see their life as a temporary mist?

2. Think about how vital water is to sustain life. Do most people view their life as vital to others?

3. Jesus brought life and restoration as the kingdom of God came. Do you bring life to all that your life touches?

4. David says, "O God, you are my God; earnestly I seek you; my soul thirsts for you; my flesh faints for you, as in a dry and weary land where there is no water" (Psalm 63:1). Do you feel like God is as vital to you as water?

5. What is one thing you can do today to allow God to use your life to bring life to others?

# Journal Pages

This is a great opportunity to journal what you are learning or the action steps you want to take based on this lesson. Doing so will keep all your notes and journaling in this book as future reference. Start by taking a few minutes to pray and ask Jesus to bring to light all you are learning and what transformational changes you can make in your life. If you are reading this in an electronic version, make a digital note and journal.

_____

_____

_____

_____

_____

_____

_____

_____

_____

_____

_____

_____

_____

_____

_____

_____

_____

_____

_____

_____

_____

_____

_____

_____

# Journal Pages

## ELEVEN

# FIRE DANCE

In many tribal cultures, there are dances and rituals that members perform to please the gods they worship. Ceremonies for rain, cleansing rituals, sacrifices, and even fire dances keep their schedules full, making sure their gods are happy.

It is easy to make our walk with God complicated. We can easily make the Bible so complicated that it is hard to tell when the writing is right-side up. The "fire dances" of the Bible keep us so caught up we can barely face God daily, not sure if we are in good standing or not. While there are a few basic principles set forth for us to follow in the Bible, they are there to ensure that we live a life that restores us to God's loving arms. They are not there to keep us performing a "fire dance," afraid at any moment that God's judgment will find us lacking in performance or afraid of failure.

God has already judged the world including us; we are worthy of nothing but death. Still, God has restored us to Him through His son Jesus. Christ's death on the cross for us is the only performance we will ever need for God's love.

God does not want our performance, nor does God want ceremonies designed to win His approval. God wants us to believe that He has our lives under His control and to live out the basics. God calls us to live out the basics and then believe that He will carry out the details of our lives.

> Jesus answered, "The most important is, 'Hear, O Israel: The Lord our God, the Lord is one. And you shall love the Lord your God with all your heart and with all your soul and with all your mind and with all your strength.' The second is this: 'You shall love your neighbor as yourself.' There is no other commandment greater than these" (Mark 12:29-31).

The simple basics are to believe in God with all our hearts, soul, and strength and to show everyone we meet His love.

Part of maturing as a Christian is to enjoy the freedom that God has everything in His control. What may have looked like mistakes in the past are springboards to put you where He wants you to be today. Nothing can go wrong and nothing can be out of control when they are God's plans.

## The Challenge

We need to stop fretting about the past and areas where we have failed. There are no complicated "fire dances" that we need to perform and no intricate balancing acts. God's plan for us is simple and the path we are to follow is basic. We need to believe that God is everything to us with finality. Second, we need to love Him with all we have and love others as much as we love ourselves. Everyone that made an impact for God in the Bible did so by getting back to the basics that God designed for them. Getting back to the basics is how God will make an impact through us. It is easy, not complicated, we need to decide today to be mature and do what He has told us.

## PONDER AND JOURNAL

Take time and ponder these questions. If you are studying this with a group, these are great discussion questions. Write your thoughts in the journal pages.

1. Do you think most people think the Bible is a complicated rule book to follow?

2. Do most people think they are good enough to get into heaven on their merit? What does the Bible say (Romans 3:23)?

3. Have you noticed Christians attempting to please God?

4. Do you feel that you have areas in your life or failures in your past that you need to make up (do a fire dance) for?

5. What steps can you take today to make God's sacrifice of Jesus on the cross final in your life for your sin and mistakes?

6. How can you love God with all that you have and love others as much as you love yourself?

# Journal Pages

This is a great opportunity to journal what you are learning or the action steps you want to take based on this lesson. Doing so will keep all your notes and journaling in this book as future reference. Start by taking a few minutes to pray and ask Jesus to bring to light all you are learning and what transformational changes you can make in your life. If you are reading this in an electronic version, make a digital note and journal.

_____

_____

_____

_____

_____

_____

_____

_____

_____

_____

_____

_____

_____

_____

_____

_____

_____

_____

_____

_____

_____

_____

_____

_____

_____

# Journal Pages

# TWELVE
# PATH

Have you ever taken a road trip? We are all on a road trip of sorts through our life. Many times that thought may call to mind images of complicated twists and turns, trying to find the exact path to take. A road or path is only a tool to help us get to our destination. The journey can be more important than the destination and is many times. The path is a way to get to where we are traveling to that has a surface that may be smoother than heading straight into the jungle whacking bushes. Depending on which path we choose to a destination may decide how quickly we arrive or which means of transport we can take the trip on. The means of transport may also decide the comfort of the "ride." On foot or a car, we might have a better chance at new discoveries, while on a plane we will miss the details. Depending on the mode of transportation, the view will be different. A path may have twists, turns, bumps, and even bridges that we must navigate. A well-groomed road has few of these challenges, allowing faster arrival at the desti-nation, though it might be a long road. There are even those times when there is no path available and bushwhacking through the jungle is the means of travel. We may not have a choice in the path we take or the vehicle by which we travel.

A bumpy, challenging road is not a terrible choice for some, as they love the adventure and the discovery. Gaining experience in travel through life on roads like this is the only choice for the adventurer. Pioneering a path is a challenging yet rewarding accomplishment. For some, pioneering uncharted territories is what they love to do. They explore the new and marvel at the discoveries as they journey through life. Their passion matches the depth of the assignment, and the stories and lessons they gain are endless.

To mature, each of us must travel some unfamiliar paths. We can do that with great delight or complete misery; the choice is ours. A smooth or bumpy road does not mean we took a wrong turn; it is just part of the journey to the destination.

Paul lived the life of a pioneer, and no doubt his path had boulders, potholes, twists, and great drop-offs. The letter with which Paul encourages the Philippians is an attitude that we should have, no matter the current path we are taking.

> Always be full of joy in the Lord. I say it again – rejoice! Let everyone see that you are considerate in all you do. Remember, the Lord is coming soon. Don't worry about anything; instead, pray about everything. Tell God what you need, and thank him for all he has done. If you do this, you will experience God's peace, which is far more wonderful than the human mind can understand. His peace will guard your hearts and minds as you live in Christ Jesus (Philippians 4:4-7).

Paul made it to the end of the journey he was on, as will we. How we progress and the attitude we have on our journey is all up to us.

The Challenge

On any journey, whether it is spiritual or physical, it is important to continue to head towards our destination. We might take a wrong turn or experience exhaustion, but continued progress towards the end of the road is essential in completing the trip. You may not be a pioneer and despise the bumpy or challenging terrain you find yourself on. Heed the advice from Paul, one of the world's best travelers, "Always be full of joy in the Lord". You will eventually get to your destination and the rest at the end will be worth the trip. While traveling, enjoy the journey!

## PONDER AND JOURNAL

Take time and ponder these questions. If you are studying this with a group, these are great discussion questions. Write your thoughts in the journal pages.

1. What does Philippians 4:4-7 say about worrying?

2. What does Philippians 4:4-7 instruct us to do instead of worrying?

3. If we follow the instructions to the Philippians, what will we experience?

4. Do you have difficulty always being joyful?

5. Does the peace of God sound like an asset you can use on your travel through life?

# Journal Pages

This is a great opportunity to journal what you are learning or the action steps you want to take based on this lesson. Doing so will keep all your notes and journaling in this book as future reference. Start by taking a few minutes to pray and ask Jesus to bring to light all you are learning and what transformational changes you can make in your life. If you are reading this in an electronic version, make a digital note and journal.

# Journal Pages

# THIRTEEN
# REWARD

Driving along one day, a car passed me in the left lane. The car was a Mercedes and as it passed the license plate caught my attention. I am often amused at what people will attach to the rear of their cars. I deciphered the customized license plate, MYRWRD. The first word was "My". The second word was cryptic. The license plate stood for, "My Reward". Plainly, the car was a reward of some type for the person who owned it. The car was nice but fell short of what I would call a reward. The owner even got short-changed on the word "REWARD" not spelled out on the license plate.

Instead, our reward is ready, waiting, and far better than a car or an enormous house at the end of life here on earth. The reward that we will receive is not a prize that will rust and fall away one day, but instead a life forever in our creator's presence. Though marriages, families, and homes may be enjoyable, the reason for living this life is more important than even those. Life is a quick sprint to run well, so we can receive the prize awaiting us in heaven. Paul explains it like this:

Not that I have already obtained this or am already perfect, but I press on to make it my own because Christ Jesus has made me his own. Brothers, I do not consider that I have made it my own. But one thing I do: forgetting what lies behind and straining forward to what lies ahead, I press on toward the goal for the prize of the upward call of God in Christ Jesus (Philippians 3:12-14).

In Corinthians, Paul asks, "Do you not know that those who run in a race all run, but one receives the prize? Run in such a way that you may obtain it" (1 Corinthians 9:24).

## The Challenge

All our life's efforts are worth the strain to reach the end of the race and receive the prize. It is so easy to fool ourselves that there is a reward that we are to be seeking while here in this life. So much around us tempts us into believing there are reward items that we should pick up along the way to heaven. There is only one prize, one race, and one effort worth aiming for, and that effort is Jesus Christ himself.

## PONDER AND JOURNAL

Take time and ponder these questions. If you are studying this with a group, these are great discussion questions. Write your thoughts in the journal pages.

1. What are some items or goals that people seek as a reward for their hard work?

2. What is the prize that Paul encourages the Philippians to run for?

3. Is it easy to tell a Christian from a non-believer by the house they live in, the car they drive, or items they buy?

4. Can you think of some ways you have gotten off-track and not ran to win the prize of heaven?

5. How can you look different by straining to reach the end of the race and receive the prize of eternal life with Jesus?

# Journal Pages

This is a great opportunity to journal what you are learning or the action steps you want to take based on this lesson. Doing so will keep all your notes and journaling in this book as future reference. Start by taking a few minutes to pray and ask Jesus to bring to light all you are learning and what transformational changes you can make in your life. If you are reading this in an electronic version, make a digital note and journal.

_____

_____

_____

_____

_____

_____

_____

_____

_____

_____

_____

_____

_____

_____

_____

_____

_____

_____

_____

_____

_____

_____

_____

_____

# Journal Pages

# FOURTEEN

## OBSCURITY

W e are all searching for significance in our lives, sometimes so much so we ignore the significant items that we have already found. Where did we learn there is a "magic" formula that once we happen upon it everything will suddenly be bright in our lives?

Many times, we treat the Bible as a soothsayer and believe that if we just hold tight to certain verses in the Bible, they will eventually wield a secret power. God's word, the Bible is true in every word, and every word that God spoke to those authors is His and hold His incredible power. What we often forget is that those words in the Bible are conditional, conditional on our obedience.

There was a boy named David born to a man named Jesse. David was the youngest of eight brothers. Being the youngest, David spent countless days in the fields watching his father's sheep. It must have been tough wondering what his life would amount to. Regardless, David spent his time in the fields tending sheep to know God intimately. Because of David's obedience and heart after Him, God used David to be King and write a large section of the Old Testament.

One day while David was watching the sheep, a brother called him to the house, and David returned to find all his brothers, his father, and a prophet of God named Samuel waiting for his return.

> Then Samuel took the horn of oil and anointed him in the midst of his brothers. And the Spirit of the LORD rushed upon David from that day forward. And Samuel rose up and went to Ramah. (1 Samuel 16:13).

One minute David was just being obedient, watching his father's sheep in the field. The next minute, David was being anointed by God as the next King of Israel.

Obscurity in the pastures was David's training ground. God chose a place for training He would have David's undivided attention. God has planned great significance for each of our lives. The challenge is allowing God to bring about that significance in His time.

Like David in the fields, it might not seem like your life is significant. If you pay attention, you will notice God has already surrounded our lives with significance and wonder. Today will never come again, and you cannot go back and make today up. God will bring the rest of the significance to your life in His timing. Until then, live this day for today; you will never get it again.

Even anointed as the future King of Israel, David went back to the fields to finish his training. David never tried to make his own way to the throne. David allowed God to give him the kingship in His time and in His way.

## The Challenge

The significance that God has planned for your life is more incredible than you can imagine. Yet, many of us are too impatient to wait on God's timing and instead attempt to make our own significance. When we short-circuit God's plan for our life, we will never know how wonderful it could have been. If David had put his own plan in place, he would have sacrificed being the King of Israel. Instead, take a moment and look at the significance your life has and all the special things which God has surrounded you. Live today for today as if you will never get it again and God will take care of all the other days.

# PONDER AND JOURNAL

Take time and ponder these questions. If you are studying this with a group, these are great discussion questions. Write your thoughts in the journal pages.

1. What does the story of David tell us about God and His plans for us?

2. Do you think most Christians make their own success or do they wait on God?

3. Do you have goals and a plan in place to assure your success? If so, how did you come up with your plan?

4. How do you see yourself compared to David in his training and waiting for God's plan for his life?

5. How can you allow God to have more influence on the plans you have for your life?

# Journal Pages

This is a great opportunity to journal what you are learning or the action steps you want to take based on this lesson. Doing so will keep all your notes and journaling in this book as future reference. Start by taking a few minutes to pray and ask Jesus to bring to light all you are learning and what transformational changes you can make in your life. If you are reading this in an electronic version, make a digital note and journal.

_____

_____

_____

_____

_____

_____

_____

_____

_____

_____

_____

_____

_____

_____

_____

_____

_____

_____

_____

_____

_____

_____

_____

_____

# Journal Pages

FIFTEEN

# CLOSE

Have you ever gotten to the point in your life where everything within you is crying out for grace? Grace is favor you may not have earned, but you need the escape? I have been there more times than I have wished and right at the point of breaking, grace comes in like a gentle wind. You may be there today, you may be there tomorrow, or your friend might cry out for that grace right now.

Not all that long ago, a mother held a baby in less than comfortable surroundings. As the birth pangs began, she wondered how she would ever get through the night. A little later, she looked down and saw the face of the grace that would save the world. Lying in her arms was the ultimate act of grace, God come to earth to save us. Imagine the creator of the universe coming to live with us, to know us, and to die for us. Imagine the grace that Mary would need as she lived through the rest of her life because she had become pregnant before she gave birth to Jesus. "Behold, the virgin shall conceive and bear a son, and they shall call his name Immanuel (which means, God with us)" (Matthew 1:23).

It was at that exact moment in history, that God came the closest to you and me. The splendid news is, He stayed with us from that point on. Many times, it feels like God is very far away, yet; the bible says it is I not God who is far away because I have strayed from God. The Bible says that God is in and through everything:

> There is one body and one Spirit—just as you were called to the one hope that belongs to your call— one Lord, one faith, one baptism, one God and Father of all, who is over all and through all and in all. But grace was given to each one of us according to the measure of Christ's gift (Ephesians 4:4-7).

In Ephesians 2, Paul tells us, "But now in Christ Jesus you who once were far off have been brought near by the blood of Christ" (Ephesians 2:13).

Perhaps one of the biggest questions in the minds of all humanity is, "Where is God, and why can I not hear Him?" By studying His words to us in the Bible, we find that He is closer to us than even our thoughts.

> Since then we have a great high priest who has passed through the heavens, Jesus, the Son of God, let us hold fast our confession. For we do not have a high priest who is unable to sympathize with our weaknesses, but one who in every respect has been tempted as we are, yet without sin. Let us then with confidence draw near to the throne of grace, that we may receive mercy and find grace to help in time of need (Hebrews 4:14-14).

These few verses explain to us that Mary's child, Jesus, was God who came to us. Because of Jesus, we are as close to God as our own skin, and nothing can separate us. If you need grace, God gave it to us once and for always through His son Jesus.

## The Challenge

Take a moment and realize that God is right there with you. God is no further away from you than the breath inside you. If you need grace today in your life as I have so many other days, take a minute and know that you can have all the grace you need. God's grace is enough because that grace is Jesus.

Do you need to extend grace to someone today? Take a minute and ask yourself how you can show Jesus' grace to someone today.

## PONDER AND JOURNAL

Take time and ponder these questions. If you are studying this with a group, these are great discussion questions. Write your thoughts in the journal pages.

1. Regardless of how we feel, what does Hebrews 4 say about finding grace when we need it?

2. Do you think Jesus can identify and sympathize with the challenges we go through?

3. Can you identify with Mary and others who are on their last ounce of physical or emotional strength?

4. What area(s) of your life do you need to draw close with confidence to the throne of grace?

5. How can you extend grace to others who need to find grace and receive mercy in their time of need?

6. What can you do to extend mercy to those you know who need it?

# Journal Pages

This is a great opportunity to journal what you are learning or the action steps you want to take based on this lesson. Doing so will keep all your notes and journaling in this book as future reference. Start by taking a few minutes to pray and ask Jesus to bring to light all you are learning and what transformational changes you can make in your life. If you are reading this in an electronic version, make a digital note and journal.

_____

_____

_____

_____

_____

_____

_____

_____

_____

_____

_____

_____

_____

_____

_____

_____

_____

_____

_____

_____

_____

_____

# Journal Pages

# SIXTEEN

# WATER

The woman walked up the path to the well again. Many times she went in the middle of the day, to avoid most of the other people in the town who went to draw water in the mornings and evenings when it was cooler. As she walked the dusty road, it reminded her of how she felt at that exact moment. In fact, it was the way she had felt most of her life. Relief for her situation was hopeless, and she would most likely live out the rest of her days in shame because of the poor decisions she had made. As she turned the corner, hoping no one would be at the well, she hesitated because on the edge of the well sat a man. She did not recognize Him, so maybe she could draw her water and not have to feel the arrows of accusation from her past failures only to get another day's pitcher of water.

The Samaritan woman continued to the well to draw water and as she arrived Jesus said to her, "Please give me a drink." The woman answered, "You are a Jew, and I am a Samaritan woman why are you asking me for a drink?" Jesus replied, "If you only knew the gift God has for you and who I am, you would ask me, and I would give you living water" (John 4:1-42).

"Please give me a drink," said the man, words that can change our lives forever. I often forget it is not what others say or think of me, but instead who Jesus says I am. When Jesus asked the woman at the well for a drink of water, He saw her for who He created her to be, instead of the mess she had made of her life. He was was offering her an opportunity to reset her life wand give her relief from a lifetime of "dusty roads."

No matter how perfectly or reckless each of us has tried to live, at some point all our paths cross Jesus'. It is only then that we realize that each of our lives has fallen extremely short and we like everyone else are incredibly thirsty for relief and grace. It is at that moment that Jesus lets down a long rope, draws water from His well, and fills our dry and dusty lives with water that quenches every longing for wholeness that we have at that moment or ever will have.

The Samaritan woman who met Jesus at the well that day had a terrible past and a very rough life up to that point. She was married five times and was now living with a man to whom she was not married. She was ashamed of her life and it was probably everything she could do to drag herself out to the well that day. Regardless, that day Jesus made an appointment with the woman and beckoned her to come to draw water so He could fill her life with Himself so she would never thirst again.

## The Challenge

If we are honest with ourselves, we are all are exactly like the woman in the story who came to draw water that day. Our lives have tremendously fallen short, and we have been searching out water that will quench our thirst from the "dusty roads" that we have been walking on. We have all searched for answers in other "lovers," either actual relationships or activities that have left us ashamed and crying out for wholeness again. Jesus sits by the well today, waiting for each of us to make that last trip down the "dusty road" of our life and allow Him to draw the last bucket of water we will ever need. Jesus knows everything we have ever done, all our needs, and He is waiting for us to ask. He will give us living water, so our roads will never be dry and dusty again.

Jesus is waiting at the well for you today; will you hesitate or run to meet Him?

## PONDER AND JOURNAL

Take time and ponder these questions. If you are studying this with a group, these are great discussion questions. Write your thoughts in the journal pages.

1. What does the conversation of Jesus with the Samaritan woman tell us about God?

2. How long of training does the Samaritan woman need before she begins to make disciples herself?

3. Do you think most people have areas of their life they have fallen short?

4. What does the story of Jesus and the woman from Samaria tell you about yourself?

5. How can you use the example of the woman from Samaria as motivation? Is there someone you have been slow to tell about Jesus?

6. Can you allow Jesus to speak to you and make you whole, leaving the past behind from now on?

# Journal Pages

This is a great opportunity to journal what you are learning or the action steps you want to take based on this lesson. Doing so will keep all your notes and journaling in this book as future reference. Start by taking a few minutes to pray and ask Jesus to bring to light all you are learning and what transformational changes you can make in your life. If you are reading this in an electronic version, make a digital note and journal.

_____

_____

_____

_____

_____

_____

_____

_____

_____

_____

_____

_____

_____

_____

_____

_____

_____

_____

_____

_____

_____

_____

_____

_____

_____

# Journal Pages

# SEVENTEEN
## PERFECT CHOICE

I f you are single, it is easy to wonder about when and who you will marry. Most people in the dating age are diligently pursuing another they find interesting. Many get eager, and there are few stories where a person patiently waited out God's choice for their mate. It is especially easy to abandon sound reasoning about the opposite sex around Valentine's Day and the holidays. It is easy to get caught up in the desire for someone to be with rather than continuing to wait for God's choice. Many get seriously involved with others they know little about or even have different religious beliefs. Most singles go through several unsuccessful dating experiences with which wisdom would have prevented. Failed dating experiences create hurt, mistrust, or even bitterness toward the opposite sex. If you are married, think about your own dating experiences. There is nothing good to gain by dating someone else's future wife or husband. Nor is there delight to think about someone dating your future spouse.

In the olden days, apart from arranged marriages, parents were vital in their children's choice of a spouse. In some cultures, children respect their fathers for their wisdom in knowing to whom and when the child will be ready for marriage. This is not including arranged marriages, but parents staying involved with their children's guidance and choices. One such example was Abraham. Abraham sent his servant to find God's choice for marriage to his son Isaac. Abraham said to his servant, "...he [God] will send his angel before you, and you shall take a wife for my son from there" (Genesis 24:7).

Abraham did not even trust his judgment for a wife for his son Isaac, but deferred the choice to God. God's choice for a lifelong mate is worth waiting for. In modern times, it is rare to see parents involved in helping their children choose their spouse. Yet, we have a Father in heaven who is very interested and active in choosing our mates for us.

The question for many is how will they know if a person who comes into our life is the "right one" or not. Since the "right one" has never shown up in each of our lives before we meet them, what shows a "green light" in a particular person over another? Good question. However, when God chooses a mate, there is no denying who the person is. God is God, and He makes His will known in marvelous ways.

God can be very much involved in the decision-making of whom we get involved with and lastly who we give our lives to. We can trust that God will help us know His will when He introduces that special person to us. We can also trust that God will confirm our choices by people He surrounds our lives with as we move into a relationship with that special person. God's choice for that special love-mate in our life is worth waiting for, and we can trust Him. He has made someone just right for each of us. To settle for anything less is, well, to settle for less.

The Challenge

God wants involvement in every aspect of our life. Many times, we substitute love relationships with others in place of the intimate love relationship that we will only find in God Himself. In doing so, we impatiently sacrifice ourselves in less perfect relationships instead of waiting out God's choice for our mate. Allow God to have complete control over the love relationships in your life and your choice for a mate, and He will bring you the person He has created just for you. Then when God presents you with the person He has created for you, listen to your heart, and those around you and you will know He has given you the love of your life. When you choose God's choice, you will not end up with anyone less than who God made for you.

# PONDER AND JOURNAL

Take time and ponder these questions. If you are studying this with a group, these are great discussion questions. Write your thoughts in the journal pages.

1. What does Abraham's choice for God to choose Issac's wife tell us about God?

2. Look at Genesis 24 and how Abraham's choice to allow God to pick worked out. Was it the right decision? How vital was the role that Issac's wife played in the lineage of Jesus?

3. Is there a difference between an excellent choice and the ultimate right choice?

4. Think about how it makes you feel about allowing God to pick your mate rather than dating to find your mate? What does this tell you about yourself and your trust in God?

5. What can you do moving forward to allow God to pick your mate rather than you?

**Parents: This is a great lesson to apply to your own life.**

1. Think back to how you found your spouse and how that way of making choices may still be in control of your life today.

2. If you are a single parent, how can you allow God to choose how you marry or stay single from now on?

3. If you have a son or daughter, this is a great opportunity to have them read the story of Issac and talk to them about dating or not to date.

4. How can you as a parent encourage your children to put God in control of their choice for a spouse?

5. How can you as a parent support and stay involved with helping your children to allow God to choose their mate?

# Journal Pages

This is a great opportunity to journal what you are learning or the action steps you want to take based on this lesson. Doing so will keep all your notes and journaling in this book as future reference. Start by taking a few minutes to pray and ask Jesus to bring to light all you are learning and what transformational changes you can make in your life. If you are reading this in an electronic version, make a digital note and journal.

_____

_____

_____

_____

_____

_____

_____

_____

_____

_____

_____

_____

_____

_____

_____

_____

_____

_____

_____

_____

_____

_____

_____

# Journal Pages

EIGHTEEN

ABSORBED

The woman walked to her car at the end of another long day at the office. The too familiar thought crept into her mind as it did every day on her drive home from work. But determined that she could ignore it once again, she drove the short distance to her home. As she turned onto her street, her eyes searched, the driveway wondering if she would spend another night alone like she did so many nights. While her eyes searched, a thought was almost audible, "Even if he was home, it will be another lonely night like countless others."

"Even if he was home," sad, but honest words spoken every day by many men and women around the world. It is hard to remember that once we get married, we are not only living for ourselves, but in the vows of marriage we have promised to turn our focus more to serving our spouse rather than serving our own interests.

Serving another person is such a tough concept for humans to understand. There have been few times in my life, outside of reading the Bible or spending time with God, when any training or teaching has centered on helping me be a better servant to others or my spouse. Never in the history of man have we been farther from knowing how to serve others.

The greatest example of a servant was Christ. He came into the world to give up His life, and through that bringing glory to God. There was not a selfish moment in His life, but instead was thinking about our best interests and making sure His every movement included us. He left that example and parallel for us, so we would know how to serve others and our spouse.

In Ephesians 5:25, Paul writes, "And you husbands must love your wives with the same love Christ showed the church. He gave up his life for her." There are no exceptions in God's teachings on how husbands and wives should serve each other; they should serve each other, giving up their lives like Christ gave His life for us. It is hard to comprehend the love that Christ showed us, and that should be the least of how incredibly we serve our husband or wife.

To put anything other than God before or in place of our spouse is the same as having an affair of the heart. Our spouses trust us with everything, and that we would lay our life and anything else down for them, no excuses.

## The Challenge

Divorce is rampant in the world today and millions are walking away from the person they promised their life to with sentences that start with, "I am not getting." Rather, they should say, "I did not give unselfishly to my marriage." It is not rocket science that no one enjoys being in a marriage where the other person is having an affair with something or someone else. We must learn as husbands and wives to serve each other in everything we do. For husbands, that may mean learning to be romantic and do scrapbooking with their wife. For wives, that could mean learning to take more of an interest in her husband's interests, or finding a hobby that they both enjoy together. Above all, learn to serve your spouse by being with them and doing things with them. A husband and wife, according to the Bible, are one person; so as married couples we need to learn how to be one. If your husband or wife dreads evenings and weekends, begin being the servant you promised them to be. As Christ loved, we must love.

## PONDER AND JOURNAL

Take time and ponder these questions. If you are studying this with a group, these are great discussion questions. Write your thoughts in the journal pages.

1. What does Ephesians 5:25 tell us about Jesus?

2. What does Ephesians 5:25 tell us about the quality of love Jesus has for us?

3. Do you think it is possible to love our spouse with the same degree of love and Jesus loves us?

4. What does reading about Jesus' love for you in Ephesians 5:25 tell you about yourself?

5. How can you love your spouse more like Christ loves the church?

# Journal Pages

This is a great opportunity to journal what you are learning or the action steps you want to take based on this lesson. Doing so will keep all your notes and journaling in this book as future reference. Start by taking a few minutes to pray and ask Jesus to bring to light all you are learning and what transformational changes you can make in your life. If you are reading this in an electronic version, make a digital note and journal.

_____

_____

_____

_____

_____

_____

_____

_____

_____

_____

_____

_____

_____

_____

_____

_____

_____

_____

_____

_____

_____

_____

_____

_____

# Journal Pages

# NINETEEN

## EXTRAVAGANT ROMANCE

The dragon drew his breath with nostrils smoking while Kristoff tried to raise himself off the ground from the last blow he took from its tail. The next exhale from the dragon will certainly be deadly flames to end Kristoff's life. With every muscle in his body exhausted and no strength left, he braced himself for the searing flames that would engulf and consume him at any second. Out of the corner of his eye, Kristoff saw movement from a familiar figure that ran directly in the dragon's path. His body found just enough strength to gaze a better look; yes, it was his love Kirsten putting herself directly in the path between him and the dragon. The flames would now consume both of them in the next fiery breath. Immediately, Kristoff found new strength in his tired muscles, and in one movement his hand had grasped his sword, raised his body to its feet, and heaved the sword into the dragon's throat, severing its air supply. In the next motion, Kristoff swept Kirsten from the shadow of the falling beast and set her feet gently down out of the clutches of danger.

Almost as much as the breath we breathe, ingrained into

our souls is romance, adventure, exploration, and discovery. God made each one of us with the stuff it takes to explore the ocean's floor, climb the highest mountain, or even discover the world's most precious jewels. Whether we actually take on those adventures is dependent on us, and where we focus our energies. It may take us a lifetime to train and develop the strength and endurance to accomplish just one of these tasks; however, if God directs us to, we have the ability.

Many of life's activities and accomplishments depend on the energy and commitment we make to carry them out. How you finish the task will be as unique and as creative as the person God made you to be. Though many are convinced by the world that they are not creative, God made each of us as creative as He is. On the sixth day of creation, while making his masterpiece of the earth and universe:

> God spoke: "Let us make human beings in our image, make them reflecting our nature So they can be responsible for the fish in the sea, the birds in the air, the cattle, And, yes, Earth itself, and every animal that moves on the face of Earth." God created human beings; he created them godlike, Reflecting God's nature. He created them male and female (Genesis 1:26-27, MSG).

In the most extravagant, romantic story ever, creative God made us in His image and likeness to be as extravagantly romantic and creative as He. That creative romance is what every person in the world longs to see, live, and be willing to die for. God gave everything, including His son Jesus, to die on the cross to romance us and show His love for us.

It may take a lifetime to train and develop ourselves to be extravagantly romantic to our spouses, our children, and the rest of the world. Yet, through God's example in Christ, He has instructed us to do so. It is impossible to get the skill without attempting to develop it. Our families and the world need desperately to see God's extravagant romance, and He can show it through our lives.

## The Challenge

Like Kristoff, many of you may feel like the world or circumstances have drained every bit of strength to be romantic from you. For others, romance may be a concept that seems only a select few have been born with, and your spouse and others around you brace themselves for the searing death of uncreative you. Let the thought of your loved ones alone help you rekindle new strength to fight and find extravagant romance for them. The world needs sweeping off their feet with the romantic love that God has displayed for them. God has chosen you, through your extravagant romance, to show the world God's glory. It may take each of us a lifetime of training to accomplish that kind of romance for our spouse, our children, and those God has put in our path. Yet, if you care about them, with one swift movement God can get you to your feet and make you like the extravagant romancer He is.

## PONDER AND JOURNAL

Take time and ponder these questions. If you are studying this with a group, these are great discussion questions. Write your thoughts in the journal pages.

1. What does Genesis 1:26-27 tell us about God and His creativity?

2. When people look at the universe, animals, and humans, do they see God's invisible attributes, creativity, His eternal power, and divine nature? Look up Romans 1:20.

3. Do you think creativity and romance are important for the human spirit?

4. What can you learn about yourself when you read, "God created human beings; he created them godlike, Reflecting God's nature" (Genesis 1:27)?

5. Think of 3 ways you can reflect God's glory by being more romantic and creative this week.

# Journal Pages

This is a great opportunity to journal what you are learning or the action steps you want to take based on this lesson. Doing so will keep all your notes and journaling in this book as future reference. Start by taking a few minutes to pray and ask Jesus to bring to light all you are learning and what transformational changes you can make in your life. If you are reading this in an electronic version, make a digital note and journal.

_____

_____

_____

_____

_____

_____

_____

_____

_____

_____

_____

_____

_____

_____

_____

_____

_____

_____

_____

_____

_____

_____

_____

_____

_____

# Journal Pages

# TWENTY
## DEAD

I was driving in the car with my friend a couple of days ago on the way to a meeting. We had been on the road for about a half-hour when I looked over to say something, and he was asleep. He was so sound asleep that he looked dead sitting in the seat. My mind flashed to images I have of people I have known who died. I thought, "What if he is dead?" I thought about the people his life affected. How the activities which he spent his time would change. Would they change?

His family would change, and the kids would miss him. Then I thought about how he was barely involved in their lives since his divorce. His business would change, and the employees would miss him. I wonder if his employees would miss him or move on to another job when the business sold? His church would miss him, well, at least for the hour each week he went there on Sunday and the money he gave to its programs. He never engaged in the church or built relationships. For 40 years of life, what would my friend leave behind in answer for all the hours and experiences he had?

The answer for many of what our life contributed to this

planet and more important, God's kingdom would not amount to much. Most live lives centered on consuming, not constructing or using that life to amplify God's glory. A life of seeking glory for themselves instead of God.

Paul in the Bible was perhaps the best example, other than Jesus, of using every ounce of effort he had in this life to make a difference for God. Paul understood that this life was not for squandering, but for magnifying our creator God and leaving a legacy behind that points only to Jesus. After turning his life over to Jesus, Paul wrote 13 books of the New Testament and spent the rest of his life leaving a legacy and glorifying God. Paul wrote:

> ...as it is my eager expectation and hope that I will not be at all ashamed, but that with full courage now as always Christ will be honored in my body, whether by life or by death. For to me to live is Christ, and to die is gain (Philippians 1:20-21).

For Paul, there was no question of why God gave him life, it was to serve Him with every second. With Paul's death, no one other than Jesus has made such a tremendous impact to glorify God.

## The Challenge

Why is it so hard to get the priorities of our life in the right order? With just light reading of the Bible, it is easy for even the common person to understand that our life is to leave a legacy for Christ. When we die, the jobs we do, and the things we can amass are forgotten or redistributed, but the life we have lived can leave a legacy that glorifies God. The only difficulty is making the final determination that, "living is for Christ", not ourselves.

The lives of the richest men in current times, from Howard Hughes to Bill Gates, are nothing compared with the amazing legacy that Paul left. Howard and others have had everything this world has to offer. However, Paul's life of meager material goods, much of it spent in prison, has left us a life to admire. The question to ask yourself is will we will remember your life as Paul's, making an impact for something everlasting and worth living, or like my friend's in the car? While we are living, we may never know the impact our life will leave for Christ, but we can live it like Paul, understanding that, "living is for Christ" and nothing else.

## PONDER AND JOURNAL

Take time and ponder these questions. If you are studying this with a group, these are great discussion questions. Write your thoughts in the journal pages.

1. What does Philippians 1:20-21 and the way Paul lived tell us about God?

2. From what you have read here, how did Paul's life differ from other Christians you know?

3. Do you think God wants our lives to make as big an impact as Paul's? Explain.

4. What thoughts and feelings do you have about yourself when you read Philippians 1:20-21?

5. Do you want to have a far-reaching impact on the world for God like Paul? If so, how can you start today?

# Journal Pages

This is a great opportunity to journal what you are learning or the action steps you want to take based on this lesson. Doing so will keep all your notes and journaling in this book as future reference. Start by taking a few minutes to pray and ask Jesus to bring to light all you are learning and what transformational changes you can make in your life. If you are reading this in an electronic version, make a digital note and journal.

_____

_____

_____

_____

_____

_____

_____

_____

_____

_____

_____

_____

_____

_____

_____

_____

_____

_____

_____

_____

_____

_____

_____

_____

_____

# Journal Pages

# TWENTY-ONE
## PRIORITY

She was across the room, and everything in the world drew him to her. It seemed like she kept looking his way. He could not keep his eyes off her and even though she may devastate him, he must know if her looks in his direction were for him. At first, he thought she might be looking at someone else. After several glances his way with her beautiful smile, he was almost certain it was he she was looking at. He would give anything if only he could talk with her.

Months later, after their first meeting when her smile drew him to her, they stepped down the church steps and into the car that awaited them to sweep them off to their honeymoon. Neither of them could believe the day of their wedding had arrived and they could now spend the rest of life building their lives together.

It was another night alone for her, not unlike countless other nights, she thought. The scattered pieces of the life they started were hard to recognize, and she wondered if it would ever fit together again. Surely everything would work out, and only a little more time and their marriage would return to perfect bliss. But still she wondered.

How many times around the world is this scene rehearsed daily? One is too many. Yet, thousands and thousands of people live in abandonment, while their spouse stays trapped in a vicious cycle of busyness. In marriage, nothing is more unnatural than for a spouse to rate lower than anything but God. God made it that way for an incredible reason. Two married people are one person. As Adam said, "She is part of my own flesh and bone..." (Genesis 2:23). Yet it is common for spouses to abandon their own flesh and bone by disconnecting daily, emotionally, and physically from their spouses. God says it like this:

> Husbands, love your wives, as Christ loved the church and gave himself up for her, that he might sanctify her, having cleansed her by the washing of water with the word, so that he might present the church to himself in splendor, without spot or wrinkle or any such thing, that she might be holy and without blemish. In the same way husbands should love their wives as their own bodies. He who loves his wife loves himself. For no one ever hated his own flesh, but nourishes and cherishes it, just as Christ does the church, because we are members of his body (Ephesians 5:25-30).

God wants and requires us to always put Him first in our lives. But then directly after Him, if married, a spouse is the next priority. Nothing should take the place of a spouse — not a job, hobby, or even ministry to others. In the Bible, God is clear about the order of our priorities. In Ephesians, God compares the priority a spouse is to the priority the Church is to Christ. God places value on ministry to others and requires it from us, but never before ministry to a person's own spouse.

Care, love, and ministry to a husband or wife, is first and chief in a person's life. A husband or wife should never be less than anything but God in their spouse's life. The only person more important to a husband or wife in their life is God. More often than not, a person's wife or husband takes a lower priority in ministry leaders' lives, and families suffer significant effects from it. It is easy for us to see the negative impact that a workaholic's family suffers; yet, we tolerate a person's life when they are driven in ministry. We see the justification in their life of service, while their family suffers much pain.

Those involved in ministry should have the greatest marriages and closest families. Many times the demands of ministry pull those involved in ministry away from their families and their family suffers. We accept that activity in "service to God" means putting family second and is part of the sacrifice a person must make to serve God. Paul warned:

> I think that in view of the present distress it is good for a person to remain as he is. Are you bound to a wife? Do not seek to be free. Are you free from a wife? Do not seek a wife (1 Corinthians 7:26-27).

> I want you to be free from anxieties. The unmarried man is anxious about the things of the Lord, how to please the Lord. But the married man is anxious about worldly things, how to please his wife, and his interests are divided... (1 Corinthians 7:32-34).

In 1 Corinthians 7:8-9 Paul continues with the same advice for women:

> To the unmarried and the widows I say that it is good for them to remain single, as I am. But if they cannot exercise

self-control, they should marry. For it is better to marry than to burn with passion (1 Corinthians 7:32-34).

Paul devotes 1 Corinthians chapter 7 to husbands and wives and is clear, their responsibilities are to their spouse first after God.

## The Challenge

If married, God is clear about the structure of our priorities, and He is always to remain first. Second, service to others is to be the next priority. Yet, if married, the second priority is to be a person's spouse. Once a person marries, they forget to make the vital switch in priorities. Now instead of others being first importance in their life, their spouse must hold that place. Though the married unit is two independent people, spiritually and in God's mysterious ways, they are the same. God loved humanity so much that He sent Jesus to live on earth for thirty-three years and die for her (John 3:16). In the same manner, married couples are to abandon everything for each other. This means "dying" to everything else, even ministry, to minister to each other first. If you are married, ask yourself if these priorities are in place in your marriage. If you are single, make a mental note to remember to make the vital switch in priorities on your wedding day.

## PONDER AND JOURNAL

Take time and ponder these questions. If you are studying this with a group, these are great discussion questions. Write your thoughts in the journal pages.

1. What does Ephesians 5:25-30 tell us about God and His love for the Church body?

2. Do you see people give their priorities to a career, a hobby, video games, or ministry? Even a long commute to work can take essential time away from a spouse and/or family.

3. Do you think it is vital for people to re-prioritize their careers, hobbies, and even watching television, putting their spouse and family first only after God?

4. Do you think many in professional ministry misplace their priorities?

5. What does Ephesians chapter 7 tell you about yourself? If you are single, are you content with being single? If you are married, are your priorities aligned with these verses?

6. Look at each area of your life and find at least three ways you can make God first, your spouse and family second, and everything else come after that.

7. How could doing life-on-life discipleship by getting together outside the church building with others to study the Bible and eat together help restructure priorities?

# Journal Pages

This is a great opportunity to journal what you are learning or the action steps you want to take based on this lesson. Doing so will keep all your notes and journaling in this book as future reference. Start by taking a few minutes to pray and ask Jesus to bring to light all you are learning and what transformational changes you can make in your life. If you are reading this in an electronic version, make a digital note and journal.

# Journal Pages

## TWENTY-TWO

## RIVER

The river was clear and gentle and welcomed contrast to the harsh dry sands the Spanish had spent weeks in before finding it. Surely, this was a place that would be good, but what is the small settlement just up ahead? Sure enough, other people had already found the river and agreed it to be an excellent area to settle down. That day in 1691, the area formerly known as Yanaguana to the Payaya Indians, which means the clear water, the Spanish would rename to San Antonio. In later years, it would be Mission San Antonio de Valero or better known as The Alamo. In 1836, The Alamo hosted the battle that would give Texans their freedom.

It was necessary, especially in the early years of a country, for settlements to establish themselves around an excellent water source. Water was the first concern for lasting survival. Today, water is as necessary and villages, cities, or any occupied area must have an excellent water source for those living in or around it.

As important as water is to us as humans, it is also necessary to have an established spiritual water source. Without a spiritual water source, survival in our spiritual life is impossible. In the early years of civilizations, finding water to establish settlements was treacherous. In contrast, finding the spiritual water which all humans thirst for is readily available.

> On the last day of the feast, the great day, Jesus stood up and cried out, "If anyone thirsts, let him come to me and drink. Whoever believes in me, as the Scripture has said, 'Out of his heart will flow rivers of living water.'" Now this he said about the Spirit, whom those who believed in him were to receive, for as yet the Spirit had not been given, because Jesus was not yet glorified. John 7:37-38

After thirsting for thousands of years in a spiritual "desert," humanity had right before their eyes the source of living water. Once they drank the water that Jesus gave them they would never thirst again. Like the physical river the Spanish found, there are already people who have found this spiritual river and settled. Yet, there is always room for more to live there. Also, like the name of the river the Spanish found, this river is the cleanest and purest spiritual water. There will be no battle fought to gain the inhabitants of this settlement their freedom because Jesus died and rose again to gain their freedom.

Throughout the ages, many have tried to counterfeit this spiritual river that God has given them and instead create their own.

> "Stand in shock, heavens, at what you see! Throw up your hands in disbelief--this can't be!" God's Decree. "My people have committed a compound sin: they've walked out on me, the fountain of fresh flowing waters, and then dug cisterns-- cisterns that leak, cisterns that are no better than sieves" (Jeremiah 2:12-14, MSG).

The river that God has provided, Jesus, is the perfect spiritual river for each of us. Instead of freedom, an attempt to make our own water or find substitute water from a different river than Him will only give us frustration and eventually death.

## The Challenge

Inside each of us, there is a small voice telling us there is more to life than we already have. We know the voice; we hear it in the mornings when we are getting ready for work, and we hear it in the evenings as we are falling asleep. We know the voice and many times decide it is something that we must overachieve to fulfill. Yet, that voice is God calling to us to settle ourselves by the only river that we will ever need. Many of us cannot believe it can be so simple, and so we spend many years searching the "desert" only to find ourselves parched and desperate for the cool, clean river. Others tell themselves that they want the river but need to get through just one more week. Without the spiritual water in our lives, which comes from a daily relationship with Jesus, we will all certainly die. Take a minute and ask yourself if you have a daily relationship with Jesus or have been trying to quench your spiritual thirst with church attendance, religious activity, or something else. Jesus, the living water, is not found through others, though they can help you find him. Only you can decide to settle next to Jesus, the river of living water.

PONDER AND JOURNAL

Take time and ponder these questions. If you are studying this with a group, these are great discussion questions. Write your thoughts in the journal pages.

1. What does Jeremiah 2:12-14 tell us about God?

2. Why are so many trying to find spiritual water in other things when God has made it easy and free?

3. Do you think people view Jesus the living water insufficient to meet their needs?

4. What do Jeremiah's words to Israel "...then dug cisterns—cisterns that leak, cisterns that are no better than sieves" (Jeremiah 2:13) tell you about yourself?

5. What does it mean to have dug wells or "broken cisterns that can hold no water?"

6. How can you answer the voice of God calling to you to leave the desert and settle yourself next to Jesus, the only river that we will ever need?

# Journal Pages

This is a great opportunity to journal what you are learning or the action steps you want to take based on this lesson. Doing so will keep all your notes and journaling in this book as future reference. Start by taking a few minutes to pray and ask Jesus to bring to light all you are learning and what transformational changes you can make in your life. If you are reading this in an electronic version, make a digital note and journal.

_____

_____

_____

_____

_____

_____

_____

_____

_____

_____

_____

_____

_____

_____

_____

_____

_____

_____

_____

_____

_____

_____

_____

_____

_____

# Journal Pages

# TWENTY-THREE
## CAGE

My mother has an African Lovebird named Tiki. Tiki likes his life indoors and has a sheltered, posh life with all the benefits. Tiki has an eight-story cage, a seed bowl that is always full, a soft cozy bed, and all the comforts of air-conditioning in the summer and heat in the winter.

As I held him one day, I wondered if he knew God. Maybe a strange thought, but do animals know who God is without question? I believe they know God; all nature must, for He is its creator. When Tiki needs something, does he ask God for it or does he simply know that God will take care of his need?

If birds have faith, then Tiki might have more faith than even other birds. Tiki needs to have faith that not only will God provide for him, but that his provision from God will come through his caretaker. He is very helpless to do anything himself, to gain what he needs in any way other than through someone else. Compared to other birds, Tiki might have an easier physical life. He always has food without getting up early to "get the worm" and even received medical attention that without he would have died.

Yet, Tiki has lost his freedom from certain natural acts. He is not free to make his own decisions on where to go outside his cage, and he has never flown. But does he care? Other birds are free as the wind, they spend their days as they want, but subject to disease, or even getting eaten. So, there are good points and bad points to that freedom. Given all the benefits of being a "caged" bird, maybe the loss of freedom is worth the other benefits. Tiki's gain of benefits comes with the loss of being able to fly and be free in the world as a natural act. If deciding on his own, knowing all the choices, would Tiki choose the life indoors or out?

Tiki's scenario is much like ours. Many view a life surrendered to God as a life put in a cage without freedom. The freedoms they feel they would lose are the freedoms that the world tells them they have rights to have. The only freedom that God requires us to give up is the freedom to sin.

When we choose God, we are deciding to let go of the freedom of sin for the gain of being with Him and all His benefits. To be in relationship with God, we give up freedoms that we could have. Those sinful freedoms would cause a life without God. Knowing all the options, a life in God with all the benefits of His provision and love, far outweighs the freedom of sin. Once we learn of God's love, it is easy to trust giving away what we may sense as freedom, and recognize it as not a loss but freedom itself.

And he said to all, "If anyone would come after me, let him deny himself and take up his cross daily and follow me. For whoever would save his life will lose it, but whoever loses his life for my sake will save it. For what does it profit a man if he gains the whole world and loses or forfeits himself" (Luke 9:23-25)?

137

The Challenge

I believe God wants us to be more like Tiki, helpless to do anything without Him providing for us. The "cage" that He provides us is not a cage to take away our freedom, but a "cage" that is for our protection. God created us to have freedom and happiness with Him, and the freedom of sin only brings sadness with a life and eternity apart from Him.

# PONDER AND JOURNAL

Take time and ponder these questions. If you are studying this with a group, these are great discussion questions. Write your thoughts in the journal pages.

1. What does Luke 9:23-25 say about us taking care of our own lives?

2. Do you think many believe God's rules and the counter-cultural lifestyle He promotes puts them in a cage?

3. Do believers you know act restricted to a cage or are the restrictions freedom and protection?

4. Can you see the Bible, God's word as an instruction book to give you freedom?

5. How can you more embrace God's instructions as a protection from sin and the world?

# Journal Pages

This is a great opportunity to journal what you are learning or the action steps you want to take based on this lesson. Doing so will keep all your notes and journaling in this book as future reference. Start by taking a few minutes to pray and ask Jesus to bring to light all you are learning and what transformational changes you can make in your life. If you are reading this in an electronic version, make a digital note and journal.

# Journal Pages

# TWENTY-FOUR
# IMMOVABLE

It was a day, similar to any other day. Nothing was unusual about the weather; the morning's news was bad as always. As he was walking to his car parked in the driveway, the too familiar feeling of despair crept back into his mind. The feeling had been with him every day since he could remember. Yet, he had gotten used to ignoring it. Once he arrived at the office and got covered up with the day's work, the feeling would soon subside. He usually worked late and could get home, eat his warmed up dinner, and get to bed before there was enough time for the feeling to return.

As he turned the corner out of the neighborhood, the feeling got worse than it usually was. He knew he only needed to think about the day and the tasks ahead, which would get rid of the feeling. As he turned each corner, the pain got worse and worse, and he wondered if he would even make it to the parking lot of the office before having to pull off the road. Ahh, the office was in sight, and in minutes he would be in the safe refuge of missed deadlines and a plethora of phone calls. As he pulled his sports car into a parking space, the tears welled up, and he sat sobbing uncontrollably. Regardless of all his success and outward appearance of having it all together, his life was in shambles. It had been for a long time. He had only reached out for help from others twice and prayed to God in extreme cases. He had been immovable toward reaching out for help from God or anyone. Now he sat in his car with nothing to show for his life but failed marriages, failed friendships, lonely nights, busy days, and a half-warmed seat in church on Sunday morning. God felt as far away as he had left Him years ago.

Much of what we teach in families, secondary school, college, and business is how to get ahead, stay ahead, and leave everything else in the dust. We have learned it well, and most have applied the teaching by leaving everything that could be dear to them in a huge plume of smoke. After destroying everything meaningful, the only thing left around these faithful learners is what they have created. Their only friends are others like themselves who have also destroyed their lives. While trying to create "life" and find a happy life, they left out the essential ingredients, God and caring for others.

Look at this story in the Bible which shows how temporal the material things in life are and how permanent spiritual decisions are:

There once was a rich man, expensively dressed in the latest fashions, wasting his days in conspicuous consumption. A poor man named Lazarus, covered with sores, had been dumped on his doorstep. All he lived for was to get a meal from scraps off the rich man's table. His best friends were the dogs who came and licked his sores.

Then he died, this poor man, and was taken up by the angels to the lap of Abraham. The rich man also died and was buried. In hell and in torment, he looked up and saw Abraham in the distance and Lazarus in his lap. He called out, 'Father Abraham, mercy! Have mercy! Send Lazarus to dip his finger in water to cool my tongue. I'm in agony in this fire.'

But Abraham said, "Child, remember that in your lifetime you got the good things and Lazarus the bad things. It's not like that here. Here he's consoled and you're tormented. Besides, in all these matters there is a huge chasm set between us so that no one can go from us to you even if he wanted to, nor can anyone cross over from you to us" (Luke 16:19-26, MSG).

Even Solomon, the richest and wisest man who ever lived, said that everything is meaningless except to fear God and obey His commandments.

The end of the matter; all has been heard. Fear God and keep his commandments, for this is the whole duty of man. For God will bring every deed into judgment, with every secret thing, whether good or evil (Ecclesiastes 12:13 & 14).

## The Challenge

Millions of people's lives around the world lie in devastation. Yet, they put on an outward appearance that they have every-thing together. They have also devastated most of the lives they have touched. Their resolve, "life is tough", continues to affect even more lives with their recklessness. They hide in a shell of successful-looking businesses, decadent houses, and a seat in church for an hour on Sundays. Like in the story of Lazarus, they ignore the genuine needs in life and waste their days here on earth focused on only themselves. They may throw an occa-sional crumb of hope towards a charity of need, but they imprison their lives in selfishness. This person has become "immovable" toward getting closer to God and lives a shallow form of Godliness. Reflect on your own life and ask the real question to whether you focus your life on God's agenda, or solely your own? You may know those who have abandoned a shallow life for a life rich in God's plans for them. It would be well worth your time to spend time with them learning about the rich life God has for you. For those heading down a dead-end life pattern, the challenge is to turn your life around and not to ignore that there is a change that needs to take place. God has an incredible plan for everyone's life, but to experience it our lives must squarely focus on Him, and give God complete control.

## PONDER AND JOURNAL

Take time and ponder these questions. If you are studying this with a group, these are great discussion questions. Write your thoughts in the journal pages.

1. What does the story of Lazarus tell us about God and His form of commerce?

2. What does the richest man who has ever lived say is the whole duty of man?

3. How do you think a person's life looks who is squarely focused on God giving Him complete control?

4. Do you know people who have abandoned a shallow life for a life rich in God's plans for them?

5. What does the story of Lazarus tell you about yourself? Is your life focused on God's agenda, or solely your own?

6. How can you assure yourself that you have abandoned everything that is not God and instead focus squarely on God's plans for you?

# Journal Pages

This is a great opportunity to journal what you are learning or the action steps you want to take based on this lesson. Doing so will keep all your notes and journaling in this book as future reference. Start by taking a few minutes to pray and ask Jesus to bring to light all you are learning and what transformational changes you can make in your life. If you are reading this in an electronic version, make a digital note and journal.

_____

_____

_____

_____

_____

_____

_____

_____

_____

_____

_____

_____

_____

_____

_____

_____

_____

_____

_____

_____

_____

_____

_____

# Journal Pages

TWENTY-FIVE

FOCUSED

She woke abruptly to the alarm clock "beeping its lungs out!" The hated alarm clock; was there anyone who looked forward to waking up to an alarm clock? Rolling out of bed, she walked over to her computer and sat down briefly to see who had emailed her in the night. Her cell phone had a new text message reminding her about a get together for the singles at her church on Sunday. She headed to the kitchen to fix the "precious brew of beans." Nothing was better than a good cup of coffee in the morning.

Back to the computer to check social media and who was on this morning. Two quick comments to friends' posts, then off to the shower to get ready for school. Where was her Romeo? Surely, the man of her dreams would show up any day now and sweep her off her feet. Yet, would she have any time for him between her friends, work, lunch dates, and weekend schedule? Hmm, she hurried off to school. Just before pulling into the school parking lot, she prayed, "God, please help me get a good grade on my test today."

In this world, everything fights for priority in our life. Work demands the most precious forty plus hours of our life. Sleep needs time, as does family, eating, and some relaxing. For singles, finding that elusive lover consumes time and energy, unlike any other activity. Only those few items take most of our time and there is little left to do anything else.

In church on Sundays, they remind us we have given little time to God during the week, except for the prayers we prayed before meals. Yet, He is God and knows our thoughts even before we think them, right? God is the most available of anyone that we should focus our time on, yet He is the most overlooked. Should God become only as available as we are to Him, or has He already? When is the last time you heard God speak to you?

Martha in the Bible had the same problem with being too busy to hang out with Jesus. She had Jesus over to her house to hang out and nearly ignored Him.

> Now as they went on their way, Jesus entered a village. And a woman named Martha welcomed him into her house. And she had a sister called Mary, who sat at the Lord's feet and listened to his teaching. But Martha was distracted with much serving. And she went up to him and said, "Lord, do you not care that my sister has left me to serve alone? Tell her then to help me." But the Lord answered her, "Martha, Martha, you are anxious and troubled about many things, but one thing is necessary. Mary has chosen the good portion, which will not be taken away from her" (Luke 10:38-42).

Martha was busy worrying about temporary things, ignoring what her priorities should be. She, like Mary, could hang out with Jesus, the very Son of God, who would buy her eternal life with His death. We too, like Mary and Martha could spend any amount of time we want, hanging out with the Trinity. Not only on one occasion like with Martha, but anytime and any day. Likewise, it is foolish beyond measure to have the writings of so many wise men compiled into a book called the Bible and to ignore them. Yet, many go about their daily tasks and relationships and never give a second thought to how basic the important priorities in life are. The world will steal away all types of time and energy from us if we let it. When instead, every day we could make it a priority to spend just a little time with the One who created us, which is worth more than any other way we could spend our time.

## The Challenge

What do you spend the hours of your days focused on and do you spend them in the best way? Tomorrow you will have at least twelve hours that you will be awake; can you spend any of those hanging out with God? Spending time with God according to the Bible should be the single most important priority in each of our lives. Jesus said:

> Abide in me, and I in you. As the branch cannot bear fruit by itself, unless it abides in the vine, neither can you, unless you abide in me. I am the vine; you are the branches. Whoever abides in me and I in him, he it is that bears much fruit, for apart from me you can do nothing. If anyone does not abide in me he is thrown away like a branch and withers; and the branches are gathered, thrown into the fire, and burned. If you abide in me, and my words abide in you, ask whatever you wish, and it will be done for you. By this my Father is glorified, that you bear much fruit and so prove to be my disciples (John 15:4-8).

Next should be the time we spend with our family. Mary recognized that nothing was more important than spending time with Jesus, and Martha spent her time worrying about only temporary things. There are hundreds of things each morning and each day that could occupy our time and priorities, God asks for only a portion of it when, as our creator, He could demand it all.

## PONDER AND JOURNAL

Take time and ponder these questions. If you are studying this with a group, these are great discussion questions. Write your thoughts in the journal pages.

1. What does Luke 10:38-42 tell us about God?

2. Is it easy to get distracted with foolish activities and waste time we could spend with God?

3. Do you think Martha thought serving Jesus was important?

4. How should we balance necessities with temporal things? After all, who would have done the serving if both Mary and Martha were sitting at Jesus' feet?

5. What does the story of Mary and Martha tell you about yourself? Are you a Mary or a Martha?

6. How can you apply the words of Jesus, "you are anxious and troubled about many things, but one thing is necessary. Mary has chosen the good portion, which will not be taken away from her" (Luke 10:42).

# Journal Pages

This is a great opportunity to journal what you are learning or the action steps you want to take based on this lesson. Doing so will keep all your notes and journaling in this book as future reference. Start by taking a few minutes to pray and ask Jesus to bring to light all you are learning and what transformational changes you can make in your life. If you are reading this in an electronic version, make a digital note and journal.

_____

_____

_____

_____

_____

_____

_____

_____

_____

_____

_____

_____

_____

_____

_____

_____

_____

_____

_____

_____

_____

_____

_____

_____

# Journal Pages

# APPENDIX

# ACCEPTING JESUS

There is a first time that each of us first encounter Jesus. You might have met Jesus many years ago, or it is possible you met Him and did not even realize it was Him. Half the world dies without ever knowing about Jesus. Along many people's everyday journey through life, they meet Jesus for the first time. It might be through a good deed, a book, a friend, or even a crisis. When the original twelve disciples met Jesus, they were working their daily jobs as fishermen. Once you meet Jesus, you must accept or reject Him, as there is no middle ground on which to stand. For some, it takes their entire life to follow Him, and for others, only the time it takes to speak His name.

The first disciples were Jews and taught from a young age of the coming Christ, the Messiah. Even expecting Jesus to come, it took many time to accept that Jesus was in person amongst them. The first disciples met Jesus on an ordinary day. He walked up to them and asked them to follow Him. To be a disciple, you must first accept to follow Jesus as the Messiah.

A good place to learn more about Jesus and the good news He brought the world is to start with the book of John in the

Bible. Those who have accepted Jesus may have never committed to learning more of Him than what others have told them. The book of John is a great introduction to Jesus and His life.

Listen to your heart as you read; what is it saying to you? Ask Jesus to show you He is the Son of God and make that real to you. If you want to meet Jesus and settle it in your heart once-and-for-always, He will show you He is the Christ. Remember, He made you, knows you, and has been pursuing you since the day of your birth. He's been pursuing each of us since the day He created Adam and Eve in the garden.

Jesus, the Son of God, died for your sins, rose from death on the third day, and will forgive you of your sins. The Bible says to be saved; a person must, "...repent and be baptized for the forgiveness of your sins" (Acts 2:38). Then you must put your trust in Jesus Christ and believe in Him, and you will be saved (Acts 16:31).

If you are ready to give your life to Jesus, start by repenting for your sins. Tell Him you are sorry for your sins and thank Him for giving His life on the cross for you. Tell Him you believe He rose to life on the third day, and He has saved you from your sins and death and that He has given you eternal life. Begin trusting in Jesus, and you will be saved. Find another Christian who can baptize you, whether in the ocean, pool, or church.

It is that simple to accept Jesus, acknowledge that He is the creator of the universe and you, and start living your life with purpose. It is by faith that we believe in Jesus, and through that faith, we are born again. Now, as we read in 1 Peter, we are "born again to a living hope through the resurrection of Jesus Christ from the dead, to an inheritance that is imperishable, undefiled, and unfading, kept in heaven for you, who by God's power are being guarded through faith for a salvation ready to be revealed in the last time" (1 Peter 1:3-5 ESV). Nothing and no one can take that gift of eternal life away from you. It doesn't mean your life gets easier; many of the disciples found more challenges to life. Jesus will transform your life like the disciples, giving it purpose and use you to tell others of Him.

Once you accept Jesus, there is only one thing left to do, follow Him, and make disciples.

Taken from *Ancient Paths, Untangling the Complexity of Discipleship*, Scott Michael Ringo

# NEXT STEPS IN DISCIPLESHIP

I often need a reminder of what success in the Kingdom of God looks like. Thankfully, I only need to look at the simple example of Jesus' discipling His twelve disciples. Jesus defined success by making disciples who made disciples. They lived, ate, hung out, had all things in common, and proclaimed the gospel message.

Success in the kingdom of God is being defined by Jesus Himself as making disciples that make disciples. From this point forward, there is no more guessing how Jesus is building His Church. True disciples are those that abide [follow] His word and glorify God by making many disciples (John 8:31, John 15:8).

We know that this is what Jesus taught the twelve disciples because this is what they do after Jesus ascends to heaven.

> And they devoted themselves to the apostles' teaching and the fellowship, to the breaking of bread and the prayers. And awe came upon every soul, and many wonders and signs were being done through the apostles. And all who believed

were together and had all things in common. And they were selling their possessions and belongings and distributing the proceeds to all, as any had need. And day by day, attending the temple together and breaking bread in their homes, they received their food with glad and generous hearts, praising God and having favor with all the people. And the Lord added to their number day by day those who were being saved (Acts 2:42-47).

We know that God approved because He multiplied their efforts, "...the Lord added to their number day by day those who were being saved" (Acts 2:47).

Disciple-making is hard work. Proclaiming the gospel message and making disciples of the kingdom of God is a life-long pursuit. Doing this work by yourself will leave you worn out. Doing the work within a community of believers who are together all the time and have everything in common, while challenging, is fun and exciting. Jesus knew exactly what to model with His disciples to train them to carry on the work in a sustainable model. The challenge is to find believers that want to be true disciples and commit their time, energy, resources, and daily life to make disciples. Being a disciple of Jesus is not going to a church building once a week to listen to a sermon, sing some songs, then waiting a year to mention Jesus to your neighbor through fellowship evangelism. Making disciples is living life together, eating together, studying the Bible, and modeling the life of a disciple.

"Immediately they left their nets and followed Him" (Matthew 4:20). The disciples who followed Jesus immediately left everything the minute they met Jesus. Then they followed Him as a community of vagabonds learning to make disciples. This ragtag group of disciples of Jesus changed the world.

Simply Scatter Seeds

This is what the kingdom of God is like.

> And he said, "The kingdom of God is as if a man should scatter seed on the ground. He sleeps and rises night and day, and the seed sprouts and grows; he knows not how. The earth produces by itself, first the blade, then the ear, then the full grain in the ear. But when the grain is ripe, at once he puts in the sickle, because the harvest has come" (Mark 4:26-29).

According to Tim Chester and Steve Timmis, "...approximately eighty-five million people in the United States have no intention of attending a church service. In the United Kingdom its forty-million— 70 percent of the population."[1] Many have walked away from the attractional church event and are looking for a more biblical model of discipleship. Yet, many have become frustrated trying to do house church or community because their training was in the attractional church and try to do what the institutional church does in a house. However, Jesus came proclaiming the Kingdom of God has come. In these verses, Jesus shows us a simple picture of how the Kingdom of God comes and grows. There are millions of people in every country looking for a gospel community of true disciples of which to be a part. Your job is to become a community of true disciples in which God can add others.

Many times farmers sow by himself. This sowing mostly happens in obscurity. The man's task is to scatter seed on the ground. After that, it grows, but that is not the man's task. His next task is to put the sickle to the harvest when the full-grain is in the ear. That harvest comes from the seed that falls on good soil. Mark 4:8 says, "And other seeds fell into good soil and produced grain, growing up and increasing and yielding thirty-fold and sixtyfold and a hundredfold" (Mark 4:8). The man harvests and brings that harvest into the barn, community.

A community of believers is not a community of unbelievers. The community in Acts was believers and God added to the community others who are being saved (Acts 2:47). The believers' position was to be in unity (John 15,) and show the world a picture of the Kingdom of God. In Mark 4:29, the farmer scatters seed. God does the growing and then the farmer reaps.

Looking further, when Jesus talks about the good soil, even when the seed is scattered on the ground, only some fall of good soil and sprout and grow (Mark 4:8).

Every person's community looks different. Sometimes our community is going to be only our family, as there is no good soil around producing a harvest. Other times we will scatter seed and much of the ground will be good soil. The key is to be consistent to scatter seed and look for the harvest. The second is to be consistent to mentor, apprentice the community God gives us.

Someone must first want to be a disciple and the seed fall on good ground. The seed must then sprout, God grows and then you gather into the community of believers. God adds to the community. If you form the community out of nonbelievers, you will have a very mixed bag of disciples as Mark 4:1-8 shows and will most likely tear the community apart.

The process to get started may seem overwhelming, especially if you are looking for others to do this with. It is hard to find people who believe in Jesus, who want to follow Him in making disciples. Even if you are part of a small group from your church, you know how hard it is to get everyone to show up weekly. It is near impossible to have participation in ongoing activities to transform the surrounding community. As easy as it sounds, getting twelve or fewer people together once a week to eat, study, and care for each other is daunting.

Married couples should start simple with each other. If you have children, it is important to include them. If you are single, start with yourself and find someone of the same gender. If you have extended family who live within a few minutes of you in town, include them. It is hard to have a community or ongoing activity if your group is fifteen minutes away from each other. It will be easier to start small and let God add to it than to start with several who are not committed. Begin studying the Bible and eating together once a week. If you are a family, commit to studying the Bible, eating most of your meals together, and helping those with need. Commit to an outreach activity and stick to it. If you are a family or close group of friends, it is easier to get a rock-solid commitment. If those in the group cannot commit from now on to getting together to study the Bible, eat together, and do outreach activities, you need to find those that will. It will never work perfectly, but discipleship is about teaching others to be like Jesus as you become like Jesus. The twelve disciples wanted to follow Jesus and learn His ways. Jesus kept them engaged, learning, and in community with each other.

## Stay Simple

The encouragement here is to start with whom you have, but make sure you build community with believers who have repented of their sins, trust Jesus, and want to do the work of making disciples, not just carry a title. Stay small until you find or make committed disciples. Stay small even after you find committed disciples. There is nothing, if not less, to gain with a large group. Read and follow the Bible and the examples of Jesus, it needs no professional education. Success as a disciple of Jesus is in making other disciples who make disciples. Jesus says, "By this my Father is glorified, that you bear much fruit and so prove to be my disciples" (John 15:8). That verse is the definition of success in the Kingdom of God.

The group you are a part of may never be large, but there are few stories of size in the Bible. The Bible is one large story of God made up of all the smaller stories of obedient sons and daughters. To make a disciple proves you are a disciple of Jesus, and that is all that matters.

# NOTES

## Introduction

1. Unless otherwise noted, all biblical passages referenced are in the English Standard Version.

## 2. Letters

1. Throughout this book I have purposely not capitalized the name of satan. I understand that it is a name and in the English language the rules say to capitalize all names. I do not consider satan to be worthy of capitalization and choose to break the grammar rule in order to not capitalize the enemy of which he is.

## Next Steps in Discipleship

1. Tim Chester and Steve Timmis, Everyday Church, Gospel Communities On Mission (Wheaton, IL: Crossway, 2012), 25.

## ABOUT THE AUTHOR

*I have food, clean water, clothes and a roof over my head today. Tomorrow can worry about itself.*

Scott Michael Ringo lover of Jesus, Husband, Father, and adventurer, is a seasoned author who writes from his experience around the world. Scott has had the fortune in life to be as the ancient explorers, living life at its fullest and always curiously looking down the unexplored, overgrown trails that lead to new beauty. Jumping aboard a schooner bound for the open sea or charting an island that needs finding, full of riches in every turn. Join with Scott and explore and discover this amazing world that God created for us to live our life glorifying Him by making disciples, while being in an intimate relationship with our passionate lover, Jesus. Scott enjoys a simple life and the simple purpose each of us has to disciple others.

## Become a world-changer

What if Jesus called us to be a disciple like he did the fishermen? Would we drop everything and follow Him?

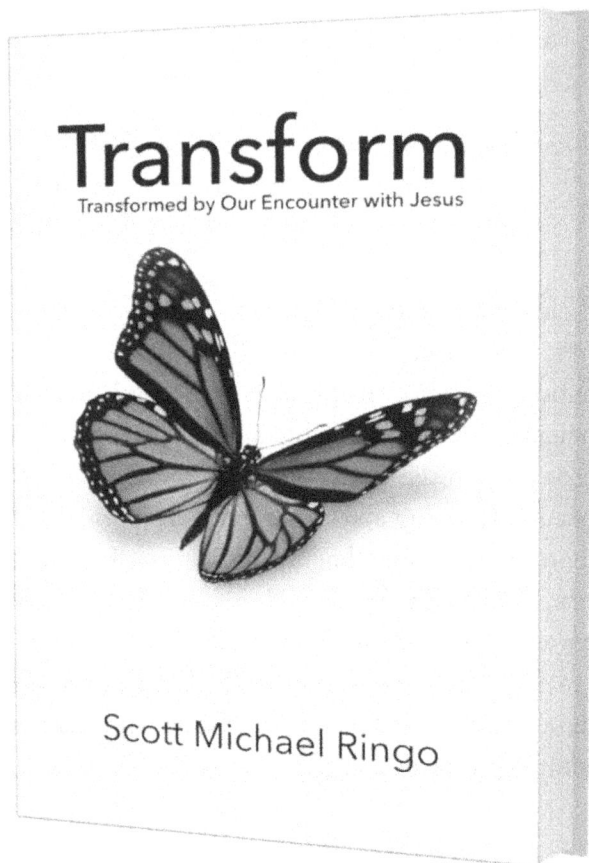

# Transform

### Transformed by Our Encounter with Jesus

## Scott Michael Ringo

Take a journey walking along the road with Jesus that once again transforms a group of disciples into His likeness, and change the face of your church, your city, or even the world.

**Available at amazon.com/author/scottringo** in print or ebook.

## TITLES BY SCOTT MICHAEL RINGO

Ancient Paths, Untangling the Complexity of Discipleship

Transform, Transformed by Our Encounter with Jesu

James, Lesson from a Fisher of Men

Simple Fundraising, Easy Non-Profit Fundraising

Explosive Marketing

Simple Non-Profit Fundraising